CN00663545

THE
SEVERN & WYE
RAILWAY

This view, taken in the early 1890s, shows S & W locomotive *Will Scarlet* standing in front of Coleford Junction signal box. The photograph provides a rare glimpse of the original box, of which, unfortunately, no details of the builder or date of provision are known. The signalman here at this time was Fred Purcell, fourth from right, who had a wooden leg, and the locomotive crew are undoubtedly William Ellaway, driver, and George Thomas, fireman. Ellaway was known as 'Uncle Locks' and was rather fond of a pint or two with the result that his fireman did most of the driving!

Courtesy Mrs. Knight

AN ILLUSTRATED HISTORY OF

THE
SEVERN & WYE
RAILWAY

VOLUME TWO

BY

IAN POPE, BOB HOW AND PAUL KARAU

WILD SWAN PUBLICATIONS LTD.

© Wild Swan Publications Ltd. and Ian Pope, Bob How & Paul Karau 1985
ISBN 0 906867 28 2

FOR
ALEC POPE

Designed by Paul Karau
Typesetting by Berkshire Publishing Services
Photo reproduction by Oxford Litho Plates Ltd.
Printed and bound by Butler & Tanner Ltd., Frome

Published by
WILD SWAN PUBLICATIONS LTD.,
Hopgoods Farm Cottage, Upper Bucklebury, Berks.

The signalman's view south from Travellers' Rest Crossing signal box on 25th June 1962. *Keith Allford*

CONTENTS

Rev. D. A. Tipper

Looking north across Travellers' Rest level crossing, with a '2021' signalled out of the 'up' loop siding, bound for Lydney.

. . . . Just after leaving Parkend station the train makes a halt among the woods and two or three coaches are uncoupled from the rear. They are bound for Coleford . . . . .

A. O. Cooke
1913

The signalman's view north from Travellers' Rest Crossing signal box on 25th June 1962.   *Keith Allford*

COLEFORD JUNCTION

The 3½ mile Coleford branch, opened in July 1875, trailed into the S & W main line at Coleford Junction, the extensive sidings here having been completed by the previous April. A reversal was necessary for branch trains from Lydney and in practice 'down' goods trains left traffic at the junction for marshalling and collection by the Coleford branch engine, whilst 'down' passenger trains were divided here. North-bound trains from Lydney usually comprised five or six carriages, the rear two of which formed the Coleford portion. On arrival at the junction these were detached and, after the Cinderford portion had continued on its way with two others from Coleford, the Coleford branch engine backed onto them. This practice could prove quite unnerving to unaccustomed passengers, one of whom clearly recalls his distress when on his first trip into the Forest he looked out of the window of his stationary carriage only to see the front portion steaming off into the darkness! A Mr. and Mrs. Wildsmith were awarded £30 compensation when, on another occasion, 26th September 1883, the brake was mis-applied on the Coleford branch engine which hit the carriages rather violently. Some passengers were thrown off their seats but none were seriously hurt. This was probably not a unique occurrence.

As mentioned in Volume 1, Parkend was the junction station for Coleford, and no doubt the platform staff were detailed to check that passengers for the branch were in the rear portion. However, whilst members of the public joined branch trains at Parkend, the workmen from Messrs. David

Another tantalizing glimpse of the old box from a carriage window in 1922.   *H. J. Patterson Rutherford*

& Sant's nearby stoneworks were able to buy tickets from Coleford Junction signal box and board the train from a special platform at the junction. By the early 1890s the S & W were issuing permits for this which enabled the workmen to travel to Milkwall and Coleford at a concessionary fare of 3d. It is not clear when this practice was established, but by June 1895 the platform had fallen into a dilapidated condition and had been removed. The workmen consequently trespassed on the line and climbed into the train while it was being divided. The Joint Committee subsequently agreed to construct a footpath and replacement platform at an estimated cost of £42. Also in July

COLEFORD JUNCTION 1906 track plan

A

A

Signal

Water Column

CANNOP BROOK

COLEFORD BRANCH

FOOTPATH

13 MILES

Weighbridge

47½ M.P.

BRANCH

ROAD

Catch Point

PARKEND

STONE SAW MILLS

Signal Box

STONE SAW MILLS

Catch Point

Signal Box

From railway road at Colliery

TRAVELLER'S REST

From Lydney Junction

From Coleford

From Coleford

To Bilson

A

A

Signal

Signal Box

Signal

Water Column

Catch Point

Tank

LINE OF PIPES FROM
BOYS GRAVE WELL

To Speech House Road

PLATFORM

FOOTPATH

From Lydney Junction

Siding

To Speech House Road

Site of Coleford Junction
workmen's platform

CHAINS

0 1 2 3 4 5

1899 the stone firm successfully applied for a reduction in fares to 2d and 2½d for their workmen travelling to Milkwall and Coleford respectively, in the evening, guaranteeing 60 tickets per week.

When the new road through the Forest was completed in 1904-5 it materially shortened the distance between the stone works and Parkend station, and the special arrangement was withdrawn around April 1906, although drivers remember workmen continuing to board here.

In April 1899 the signal engineer reported that repairs to the signal box had become necessary and that facing point locks and connectors were in need of replacement. It seems likely, therefore, that the £932 authorised in May for renewal of signals at Coleford Junction, Lydney, Severn Bridge and Sharpness, included the complete replacement with GW signals, but details are unclear. A further £30 was also authorised for improved signalling here in July 1910.

In 1899 the provision of a runaway siding at the junction was also considered, to protect the main line from breakaway vehicles or out of control trains from Coleford descending the 1 in 30 and 1 in 31 gradient into the junction. After discussion, the heavy expenditure was felt unnecessary as there had been no incidents for the thirty years the branch had been open. Instead, no trains were allowed to leave Speech House Road station in the direction of Coleford Junction while a train was working in either direction on the Coleford branch until it had come to a stand at Coleford or Coleford Junction home signal.

This was by no means unique on the S & W, no train being allowed to leave Coleford Junction for Speech House while another was *en route* from Drybrook Road until the latter had been brought to a stand in the loop siding at Speech House Road.

Two views of the yard of the Parkend stone works. The history of the concern is dealt with in Volume 1. The upper view, looking south, shows the overhead gantry crane loading wagons standing on the company's siding, and a mobile steam crane beyond. The lower scene is looking the opposite way through the yard. Beyond the gantry crane can be seen the 'tripod' crane so common in Forest stone concerns. *Gloucester Public Library*

No. 2044 taking water at Coleford Junction in 1948 before departing for Coleford. Few trains ever passed without water being taken here, with the limited capacity of the ubiquitous '2021' class saddle and pannier tanks, particularly as the Serridge supply could not always be depended upon.

Rev. D. A. Tipper

The guard's view over a train of colliery empties at Coleford Junction on 26th March 1948. The line on the extreme right is the Parkend Royal branch.
L. E. Copeland

The water crane and supply tank on 26th July 1963. The tank's more recent appearance, mounted on steel girders supported on what appear to be concrete blocks, makes this a certain replacement. However, the date of its provision, and details of the one it replaced, are not known. Furthermore no photograph has been found of the water column shown on the 1906 track plan and listed in the S & W General Appendix as being situated alongside the 'up' loop siding. It may have been removed because there was an alternative at the end of the 'up' platform at Parkend station.
Keith Allford

Looking south over the junction from the 'down' starting signal on 19th April 1946. The lines were, from left to right: 'up' loop siding, 'up' main line; 'down' main line; two loop sidings used to hold wagons to and from Parkend Royal Colliery, the stoneworks, the Coleford branch and Bicslade siding; a shorter dead end siding mainly used for Coleford traffic; and finally the Coleford branch with the extensive 1929 sand drag alongside. The 'up' loop siding at one time incorporated a wagon weighbridge of 20 tons capacity which was used for traffic from the stoneworks and possibly the Parkend Royal Colliery, whose branch can be seen running in from the left. The weighbridge was reported as being 64 years old in January 1938 when the Joint Committee recommended its removal due to insufficient use to justify the annual maintenance charge of £6 5s 0d, weighings in the district being performed at Lydney. It was removed the following year. Wagons going north of the junction were mainly empties for the collieries or goods for Cinderford. *L. E. Copeland*

Another '2021' class pannier tank taking water at the head of a northbound train of colliery empties, bound for Mierystock. The wagon and brake van immediately behind the locomotive form the Cinderford goods portion. *Rev. D. A. Tipper*

The Great Western was responsible for signalling the S & W to the north of, and including the north end of, Coleford Junction and this ground level signal cabin, so obviously a product of the GWR signal department at Reading, was provided second-hand on 1st December 1925, having come from Spythy Lane near Swansea. It replaced the original structure in a new position at the throat of the layout, the token catching apparatus presumably having been formerly situated opposite the old cabin. This photograph, taken on 14th April 1933, also shows what is possibly one of the three yard lamps provided in 1917. *L. E. Copeland*

In January 1904 twenty-five shillings was authorised for a stop board near Futterhill sidings on the Coleford branch. It read 'All goods and mineral trains must stop here', and ensured that trains were brought under proper control before descending the steep grade into the junction. However, despite the Joint Committee's apparent reluctance, a 115 yard sand drag was eventually provided at the foot of the incline immediately in advance of Coleford Junction up branch home signal, which was moved 217 yards further from the box on the 'down' side of the line. Authorised in July 1927 and costing some £840, the new arrangement was brought into use on Monday, 23rd January 1929.

The gravity fed water supply at the junction was vital, and in May 1885 G. B. Keeling reported to the Board that it was failing. To counteract this he proposed laying pipes to the source at Boys Grave Well, about a mile away. The Severn & Wye were then asked by the Crown's deputy surveyor in Dean, Sir James Campbell, to obtain permission from the Crown before doing this. Although not really agreeing with the need to do this, the company duly wrote to the Office of Woods.

The letter, dated 19th May 1885, stated that the water course from the Boys Grave Well to the Coleford Branch Junction near Parkend 'is of very little service at present as the water is absorbed by the ground before it reaches Parkend where it is required for the use of our locomotives.' It continued, 'we should be much obliged if you will kindly give us permission to lay a line of pipes for the whole of the distance so as to conduct the water from Boys Grave Well without loss to the tank at Coleford Branch Junction'.

Signalman George Cooke on duty on 15th July 1964. *A. K. Pope*

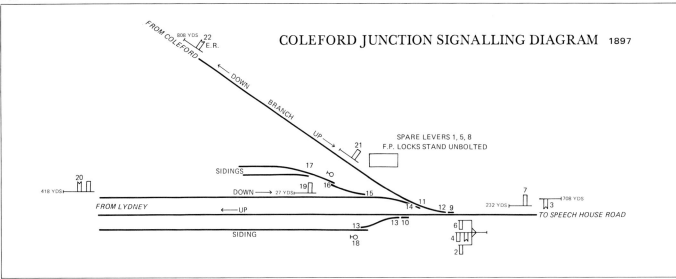

COLEFORD JUNCTION SIGNALLING DIAGRAM 1897

FROM COLEFORD

808 YDS 22
E.R.

DOWN BRANCH

UP → 21

SPARE LEVERS 1, 5, 8
F.P. LOCKS STAND UNBOLTED

SIDINGS 17

16

20

418 YDS

DOWN → 27 YDS 19

15

11
14 12 9

7

232 YDS

3 708 YDS

FROM LYDNEY ← UP

TO SPEECH HOUSE ROAD

6

SIDING 13 13 10

4

18 2

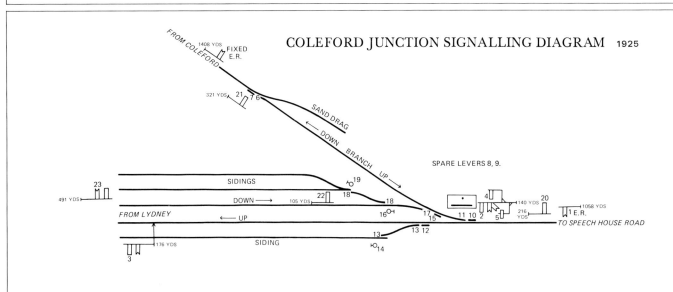

COLEFORD JUNCTION SIGNALLING DIAGRAM 1925

FROM COLEFORD

1408 YDS FIXED
E.R.

321 YDS 21 7 6

SAND DRAG

DOWN BRANCH UP →

SPARE LEVERS 8, 9.

SIDINGS 19

18

23

491 YDS

DOWN → 105 YDS 22

18

4

140 YDS 20

216 YDS 1058 YDS

FROM LYDNEY ← UP

16 17
15

11 10

2 5

1 E.R.

TO SPEECH HOUSE ROAD

SIDING 13 13 12

3 176 YDS

14

The block instrument shelf in the 1925-built signal box at Coleford Junction. The left-hand instrument is an MR pattern 'pegging' block for trains from Travellers' Rest box, that on the right applying to 'up' trains to Travellers' Rest. The MR pattern block bell between the two completed the set. Above the instruments hung the box diagram. To the right of the shelf bracket lay a couple of lever collars. *Keith Allford*

Coleford Junction box. Signalman George Cooke at the frame of the 1925 box. *A. K. Pope*

Coleford Junction box was on several telephone circuits, as this view reveals. Below the block was the booking desk, on which was laid out the Train Register Book in which all routine bell signals, and any out of the ordinary events, were recorded. *Keith Allford*

A sunny portrait of the signal box on 17th May 1961.

Keith Allford

The Crown then appears to have researched the matter, as their reply in August 1885 stated: 'it appears that four other watercourses exist for which the Company (the S & W) pay no acknowledgement. It is proposed to charge £1 per year in each of these five cases.' The other watercourses in question were those at Parkend (Volume 1, page 137), Speech House Road and Serridge Junction. It would appear that the Crown were attempting to charge for both the stream and the pipes at Coleford Junction, to which the Severn & Wye replied, 'the new watercourse is in substitution of one already used and one other (Speech House Road)

The southern end of the box, showing the tiny entrance porch.

Eric Parker

will no longer be required therefore the total acknowledgement will be £3 per annum which we are prepared to pay.'

On 21st September 1885 Keeling again wrote to the Crown, 'I am apprehensive from a recent examination of the Boys Grave Well whether the supply (after long dry seasons) will be sufficient. I am therefore desirous to add a branch connection to another spring in Brookhall Ditches, to be used only as required as an auxiliary'.

At a Severn & Wye board meeting of 12th October 1885 'the seal was ordered to be affixed to a licence from Mr. Cully, Commissioner of Woods and Forests to use and maintain certain watercourses and pipes in Dean Forest at a rent of £4 per annum'.

The reason for the charge of £4 rather than the previously mentioned £3 was that the Crown looked upon the branch pipeline to Brookhall Ditches as a separate watercourse.

The matter then rested until March 1906 when the Joint Committee wrote to the Crown to discover under which lease they paid for the water used at Coleford Junction 'which runs from the Cannop ponds by way of the brook which also serves the Forest of Dean Stone Firms.' The Crown replied that the Railway Company's water was piped under the stream, which in fact was the old leat to Parkend Iron Works, from Boys Grave Well. On investigation the railway discovered that at some time the Boys Grave supply had obviously failed, as foreseen by Keeling in 1885, and advantage had been taken of the plentiful supply along the leat. The Severn & Wye had illicitly tapped into it!

In April the committee considered increasing the reserve from Cannop Ponds by raising the dam wall by 4 feet. The outcome is not clear but in April 1908 £285 was authorised for improving the locomotive water supply at Coleford Junction and Parkend.

Looking north-west at the box on 7th June 1960. By this date the token catching apparatus opposite the box had been removed, the operation no doubt being performed by hand. *A. K. Pope*

The short-lived Coleford Junction workmen's platform was situated in the left foreground of this view. According to the 1897 signalling diagram, this down home wooden posted bracket signal replaced a triple bracket on the opposite side of the main line. The one illustrated served the same function, the small bracketed centre pivot arm near the base of the post controlling entry to the 'up' loop siding, the home and distant on the main post serving the up main and the right hand bracket entry to the Coleford branch. The boarded area in the foreground was used for the PW motor trolleys kept in the sheds to the right of the picture. The photo was taken on 19th April 1946.
L. E. Copeland

Looking towards the junction from the New Road overbridge, shown on the opposite page, on 22nd June 1947.   *L. E. Copeland*

A less elegant replacement for the signal described on the previous page.   *P. J. Garland*

This substantial bridge just north of the junction was built by the Crown when they constructed the 'New Road' through the Forest from Parkend to Mierystock. In October 1902 the Crown authorities arranged to purchase the necessary girders second-hand from the Great Western and in the following January a suitable pair were found lying at Swindon. They were charged at £5 per ton and had a total weight of about 24 tons. It was stated that the bridge was to have a clear span of 38 ft and a height of 14 ft 3 ins. In the original estimate for the road, the bridge at Coleford Junction, together with one at Wimberry, were costed at £1,500, but in February 1903 the cost of the Coleford Junction bridge alone was £1,428 11s 7d. This increase, since the preceding month, was due to the requirements of the railway who wished the span to be increased to 43 ft or 45 ft to enable the future provision of a runaway siding off the Coleford branch should one be required by the Board of Trade. When girders for this increased span were inspected at Swindon that July, it was found that both needed to be shortened and it was agreed that they would be cut at each end to remove areas of bad corrosion. In November 1903 £6 10s 0d was paid to the Great Western for the movement of a signal made necessary by the construction of the bridge together with £4 2s 0d for removing telegraph poles and wires. The bridge is pictured here on 21st August 1964. *A. K. Pope*

The opposite side of the bridge with the short post of the advanced starting signal in the foreground. *A. K. Pope*

Looking north from the road bridge with the down advanced starting signal still in use, and ferns beginning to reclaim the Crown land. *P. J. Garland*

A closer view of the old cast iron S & W gradient post shown in the foreground of the previous view. *L. E. Copeland*

An idyllic study near Bicslade with the Coleford Junction up distant (by now fixed at caution) in the foreground shadows on 21st August 1964.
A. K. Pope

L. E. Copeland

Bicslade wharf from the south, with the middle ground frame in the foreground, on 19th April 1946.

No doubt the wharf was quiet through much of the working day and this is certainly the case on this occasion when viewed from a passing train of colliery empties bound for Mierystock on 26th March 1948.   *L. E. Copeland*

BICSLADE WHARF

Prior to the abandonment of the Severn & Wye main line tramroad in 1874, Bicslade Junction, as it was then known, marked the point at which the Bicslade branch tramroad joined the main line. Whilst the date of the establishment of a railway siding at Bicslade has not been discovered, the Severn & Wye engineer in October 1871 reported that it would soon be necessary to put in a siding there for the accommodation of the stone trade.

This had almost certainly been done by the time the main line tramroad was removed, the 1877 survey of the line showing a loop siding alongside a wharf, but by 1898 there was only a single connection, which necessitated tow roping when shunting. All empty wagons for the siding had to be hauled to Speech House and brought back on special trips. Also, because of increasing traffic, the engine had often to run specially for a second clearing of the siding. It was therefore decided to provide an additional connection to the running line, and this was in hand by January 1902. By 21st April the main line had been slewed and the earthworks were approaching completion and by 8th October the work was complete.

The new arrangement, serving an extended loading bank, provided two new crossovers, one either side of the existing connection. Controlled by two new 2-lever ground frames (and the existing one) locked by the train tablet, the new work was inspected by the Board of Trade who reported:

The GW & Midland companies as owners of the S & W Joint Railway hereby undertake that all traffic taken out of the loading bank siding at Bicslade Junction shall be worked by trains having the engine at the lower end, and that in the case of wagons required to be placed in the siding by trains travelling in the direction of Speech House Road, the trucks shall be placed in the siding in full train loads with the brake van in the rear, or, in the case of through trains be formed behind the van of the through section of the train with a second brake van in the rear, the rear van and wagons being backed into the siding.

Thereafter Bicslade wharf was usually served from Coleford Junction, trains being propelled with a brake van leading 'down' the main line. According to the crews, this was easier than leaving an 'up' train on the main. This duty usually fell to the Coleford branch engine, between Coleford trains. Wagons for Bicslade were often conveyed from Lydney by the first train to Coleford and left in the sidings at the junction until required. Incidentally stone was frequently received at the wharf by rail, presumably for cutting and dressing at the works.

In July 1899 the Parkend Deep Navigation Colliery Co. Ltd. had contemplated building new screens at Bicslade instead of continuing to load coal at the dock. The proposed sidings would have left the main line at the south of the existing sidings and run alongside part of the Bicslade tramroad to the old Union pit where three sidings would have served the screens, together with a single wagon storage road. However, the Crown pointed out that as the new Lydbrook to Lydney road was in progress, a substantial bridge would be required over the siding at a cost of about £300. In March 1901 the colliery company were said to be 'thinking about it' but by 22nd April it was reported that they were not to proceed.

One of the most striking features of Bicslade wharf was its distinctive cranes. The earliest mention of these was in August 1878 when the engineer explained the circumstances under which E. R. Payne, quarryman, had been allowed to erect a crane at his own expense on the company's wharf

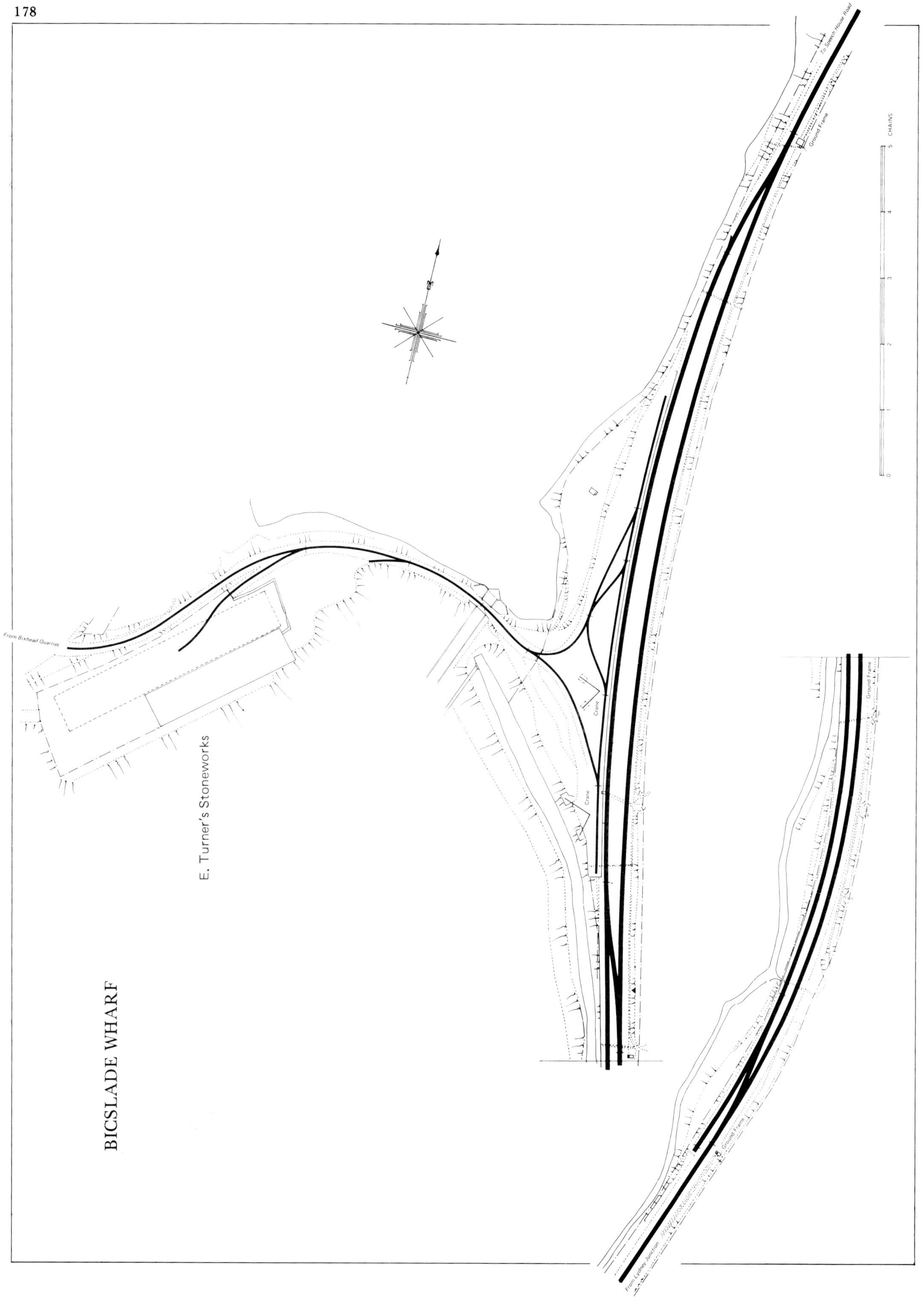

BICSLADE WHARF

E. Turner's Stoneworks

From Bixhead Quarries

To Speech House Road

Ground Frame

Ground Frame

Ground Frame

Ground Frame

To Speech House Road

From Lydney Junction

Crane

Crane

0 1 2 3 4 5 CHAINS

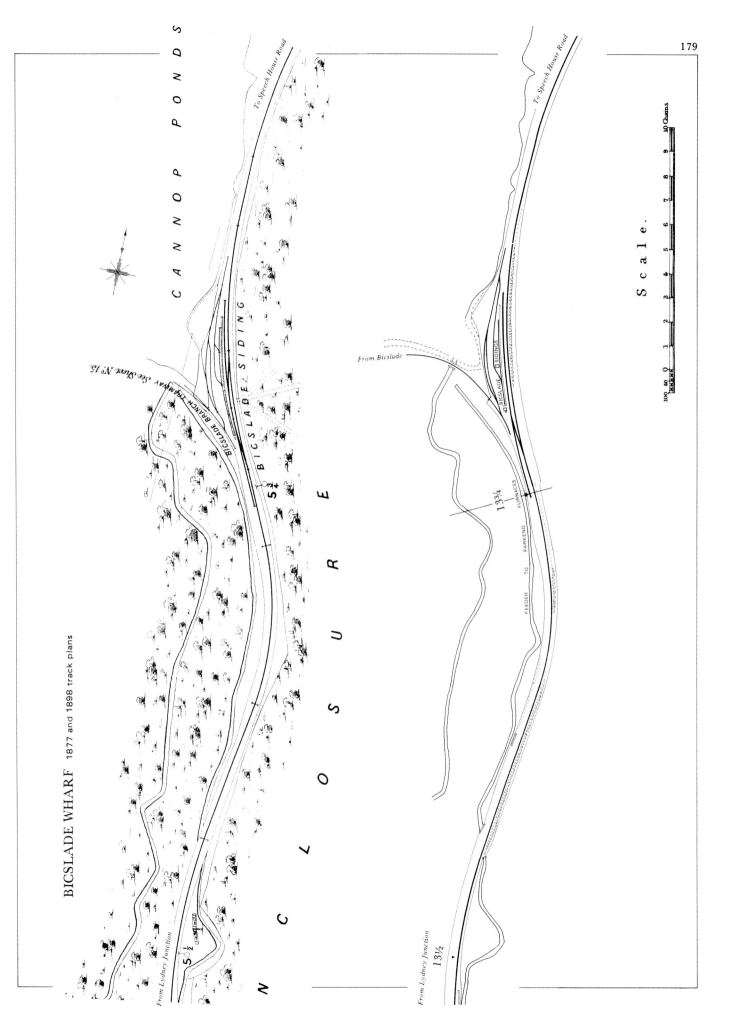

BICSLADE WHARF 1877 and 1898 track plans

As with all of the Forest industries, the output from Bicslade dwindled, particularly in the post-war years, yet life continued with little change. There was a reassuring permanence about the very existence of the old railway system and few could have really thought it would all disappear so soon, leaving the Forest strangely quiet. This portrait taken in 1948 captures a tranquil moment as No. 2044 and train crew bask for a moment in the midday sun.

Rev. D. A. Tipper

A pre-war scene featuring two of the numerous United Stone Firms' wagons waiting to be loaded in June 1939. Behind we have a rare view of a Richard Thomas wagon.
*L & GRP
courtesy David & Charles*

at Bicslade. There was no written agreement but it was understood that Payne would allow other freighters to use it on payment of 'the usual charges'. However, at this time Payne removed the handles and otherwise rendered the crane useless to other parties, so the S & W intervened, insisting that he should discontinue the obstruction.

By October 1900 Payne's crane had deteriorated and was described as being in defective condition. The largest trader at this time, Messrs. Turner & Son, were prepared to erect 'a suitable crane' which this time Payne's would be permitted to use when required by arrangement. A second 10 ton crane was erected on the wharf around the same

Tramroad wagons on the loading bank on 2nd June 1951.

L & GRP, courtesy David & Charles

The tramroad entered the wharf at right angles to the railway, crossing the narrow bridge over the spillway on the edge of the huge Cannop Ponds. Reference to track plans shows that the right-hand spur inside the gate was added some time between 1898 and 1902 when the boundary fence and gate were also repositioned. This picture was taken on 19th April 1946. *L. E. Copeland*

This team of horses and a bogie stone wagon were photographed close to the stoneworks in 1939. The stone block weighed approximately 8½ tons. This may appear a rather quaint spectacle to modern generations, yet despite its archaism such a long-lived tradition was not questioned at the time. *Collection A. K. Pope*

The entrance to the stone works with steam-operated overhead crane beyond.

Collection E. Gwynne

time by Messrs. David & Sant, and there is mention of E. R. Payne erecting another and paying rent from 2nd June 1903. However, this is not at all clear as photographs and plans only show two such cranes. By April 1901 Turner's had decided to erect near the loading bank 'sheds and machinery etc. for preparing stone brought down from the quarries', but this is detailed later. With this extra activity the Joint Committee authorised the previously mentioned extension to the loading dock at Bicslade estimated at £1,013.

Around April 1906 two blocks of stone fell from one of the traders' cranes and endangered the main line. Either the Joint Committee had always feared such an occurrence or they were simply quick to respond, for it was immediately agreed to slew the main line further away from the siding by a distance of approximately 10 ft for an estimated £145. The work, which was completed in October, appears to have been the last development at the site.

BICSLADE STONE WORKS

In late 1900 Messrs. E. Turner & Sons, quarry owners of Cardiff, were negotiating with the Crown for the lease of a quarry at the top of Bicslade. The rough hewn stone was to be brought down the tramroad and loaded onto the railway at Bicslade wharf. In order to avoid the cost of transporting unwanted stone, Turner's wished to erect a stone works close to the wharf.

On 21st January 1901 their application for a 'piece of land to use as a yard near Bicslade siding' was under consideration by the Crown. Turner's stated at this time that they were anxious to get the machinery erected as soon as possible and, to enable this, there was a good deal of levelling and filling of the site to be done. By 29th January the

GRC & W Co. wagons. The 7-plank open would have been used to bring coal to feed the boilers at the stone works. *GRC & W Co.*

Crown agreed to lease two roods of land for 20 years at £2 per annum and stipulated that the site was to be fenced all round and a screen of trees planted to hide the works from the new Parkend-Lydbrook road. Turner's agreed to the terms on the 31st as long as they could commence to erect their machinery immediately.

The completion of the lease was, however, held up for a period when the Crown discovered that Turner's intended to make a loading bank, served by a short tramway, just outside the area of land covered by the lease. Further problems arose when it was found that the yard had been built above an old level, Miles Level, used to drain the Parkend Deep Navigation Colliery Co.'s interests in Bicslade. The Parkend Co. were worried that the vibration of the machinery in the yard would bring down the masonry arch in the level which, it would appear, was already in a defective state. The Crown wanted to insert a clause in the terms of the lease, making Turner's responsible for the cost of repairs to the level. Not surprisingly, Turner's immediately objected to being held responsible for damage to a level they were not even aware of, especially as it was already defective and could fall in of its own accord at any time! It was also pointed out to the Crown that, ironically, Turner's had originally asked for a piece of ground on the opposite side of the tramroad, well away from any level, but the company had been made to take the land now occupied.

In November 1902 Turner's stated that their operations in the yard over the last twelve months had not affected the level and, following an inspection once more by the Parkend Co., the clause was dropped.

It was now the turn of the Joint Committee to enter the debate. They pointed out that part of the works was built on the original course of the Bicslade tramroad, on land which they were still renting from the Crown. The result of this was that of the £2 paid to the Crown per annum, 4/9d went to the railway.

As has been seen with the Parkend stone works (Volume One), the major stone firms in the Forest were taken over by United Stone Firms in 1910 for the sum of £31,500. They in turn were taken over by United Stone Firms (1926) Ltd. and in 1939 the Forest of Dean Stone Firms Ltd. gained control of the Bicslade works, and still operate there today.

The sandstone from the works is used for monumental and building purposes, many notable buildings being supplied with either 'Bixhead Blue' or 'Barnhill Grey', names which derive from the quarry concerned.

THE BICSLADE TRAMROAD

The branch tramroad up to the quarries at Bixhead was completed soon after the main line tramroad, being ready for use by June 1812. It climbed up the valley for all its length of three-quarters of a mile, and as well as serving the quarries at its head the line also picked up traffic from several collieries en route.

The tramroad proper, owned and maintained by the Severn & Wye, and later the Joint Committee, terminated just short of the Bixhead Quarries. The lines within the quarries themselves were provided by the traders although the Severn & Wye often supplied the tramplates.

A view in the opposite direction to that on the previous page and taken prior to 1914.   *Gloucester Public Library*

Looking west through the works yard in the 1950s when a rail-mounted steam crane served the area beyond the reach of the overhead gantry. *R. Dagley-Morris*

This view of the stoneworks on 22nd June 1947 shows the diverted Bicslade tramroad, the original course of which had run through the land subsequently occupied by the works. *L. E. Copeland*

The still beauty of Cannop Ponds secreted from the bustle of the coal trains by mature afforestation. The ponds were man-made, using the Bicslade tramroad embankment as a dam, in 1825. They supplied water to Parkend Iron Works via a leat.   *Collection Ian Pope*

Turner's stone works, by now in the hands of the Forest of Dean Stone Firms Ltd., pictured here on 22nd June 1947, is still situated alongside the ponds which ensure a plentiful supply of the water so vital to cutting operations. The ponds also provided a fitting and well-earned reward for teams of horses emerging from the secluded path of the tramroad with their heavy burden.   *L. E. Copeland*

Looking down the Bicslade tramroad in later years with the two rows of tramplates snaking between the ferns and often shaded by a canopy of trees.   *L. E. Copeland*

The branch became a feeder to the railway when Bicslade siding was laid after 1871 and became an isolated stretch of tramroad when the main line tramroad was abandoned in 1874.

At first a considerable tonnage of stone and coal was brought down the tramroad, up to 70 tons per day in 1841, but in May 1901 the Joint Committee stated that it received very little traffic. In August 1901 they threatened to add a charge of 6d per ton on traffic from Bicslade siding which had passed over the tramroad, traffic over which was still carried in, or on, traders own wagons and hauled by their own horses. This new charge would, therefore, have been a toll for using the line. The traders complained, stating that the rate from Bicslade siding had always included the rate for the tramroad. The protests were so vociferous that in November the railway was reconsidering its decision. Traffic continued to be brought down the tramroad into the 1940s, the last load of stone being conveyed on 25th July 1944, although coal was carried until November 1946.

The portion of line from the stoneworks to the wharf remained in use into the 1950s for the movement of stone between the two points. The wagons of stone were moved around using tractors, although manpower was also much in evidence.

The trackwork within Bixhead Quarries also continued in use for the internal movement of stone but supplies were taken to the stoneworks at Bicslade wharf by lorry; indeed it was vehicular traffic over the upper portion of the tramroad which damaged it beyond repair after 1947.

One of the deep Bixhead quarries at the top of Bicslade.
L. E. Copeland

Looking east and back through the gate onto Bicslade wharf in June 1947.

B. Baxter, courtesy R & CHS

A closer view of the base of one of the cranes on the wharf during its final years.

R. Dagley-Morris

Two last views of the wharf on 22nd June 1947 and 19th April 1946 respectively, showing clearly where the running line was slewed away from the loading bank in 1906 as a safety measure.

L. E. Copeland

These two views show the Speech House Road 'down' distant which was fixed at caution (together with its counterpart in the 'up' direction and those at Serridge, 'Coleford' [presumably Junction], the Parkend 'up' distant and the Travellers' Rest 'up' outer and inner distants) in August 1947. *Keith Allford & A. K. Pope*

SPEECH HOUSE ROAD

HOWLERSLADE (CANNOP) SIDING

This siding, serving an interchange wharf with the Howlerslade tramroad branch, was probably provided after 1874 when an application from Messrs. Trotter, Thomas & Co. for a short branch from the S & W main line 'to their New Road Colliery on the Howlerslade branch' could not 'at present be entertained'. A further application, in March 1875, was 'deferred for future consideration', but the siding certainly existed by 1877 when it was shown on the S & W survey as having a loop on it. A stone works had also been established on the wharf by Trotter, Thomas & Co., who owned quarries at the heads of both the Howlerslade and Wimberryslade tramroads. The works were served by a spur

off the Howlerslade tramroad and an 1889 description of them lists the machinery as comprising three horizontal saw frames; one large machine to plane landings, steps, cills and pavings; and one 'exceptionally large' circular saw.

Trotter, Thomas & Co., who were bankrupt by August 1891, amalgamated with other quarry owners the following year to form David & Sant Ltd. As already explained at Parkend and Bicslade, David & Sant were acquired by the Forest of Dean Stone Firms Ltd. in 1900.

In 1906 the south end of the wharf, a short length of tramroad and the siding, which by this time was known as Cannop siding, were extended to enable Messrs. E. R. Payne

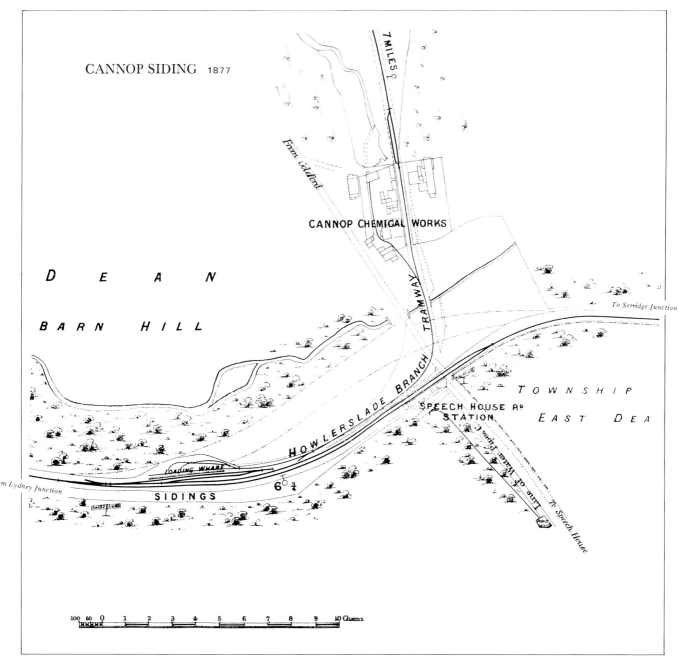

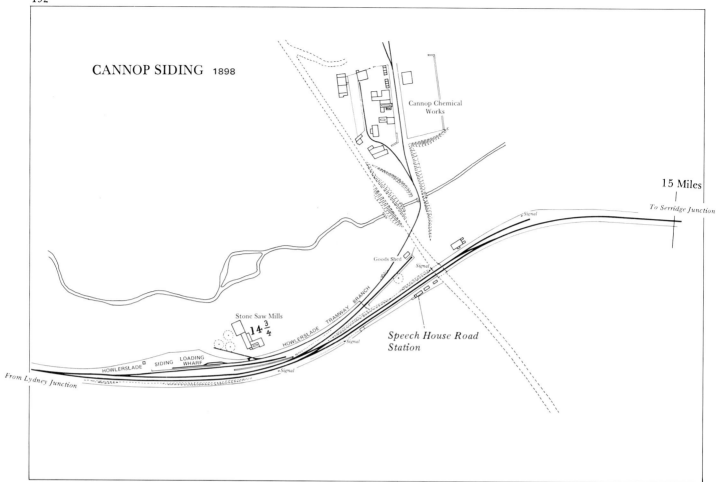

CANNOP SIDING 1898

Cannop Chemical Works

15 Miles

To Serridge Junction

Signal

Goods Shed

Signal

Stone Saw Mills

14 3/4

HOWLERSLADE TRAMWAY BRANCH

Speech House Road Station

Signal

HOWLERSLADE SIDING LOADING WHARF

Signal

Signal

From Lydney Junction

& Son to erect a crane for loading stone which was carried from their quarries along the Howlerslade tramroad. The work, costing the Committee £81, was completed in June, Payne's renting the site for their crane from 30th March. When, in 1909, the interests of the Forest of Dean Stone Firms Ltd. were up for auction, the equipment at the Cannop stone works included an overhead crane of 20 tons capacity. The works, together with the interests of E. R. Payne, were purchased by the United Stone Firms Co. Ltd.

In February 1910 the Joint Committee gave the new owners permission to use land at Speech House Road for a wharf or depot for dressing and storing stone, presumably as an extension to the works. At the same time permission was granted to erect a gantry crane for the purpose of transferring traffic between the works and the siding. The land to be used was not to interfere with the wharf, tramroad or existing crane.

The stone concerns in the Forest went through a bad patch during the First World War and, as has already been seen, the United Stone Firms went into liquidation in 1917. It continued under the receiver until 1925 when United Stone Firms (1926) Ltd. was formed. It is believed that the works closed about this time, possibly not being worked by the new company.

THE HOWLERSLADE TRAMROAD

The Howlerslade branch was not completed as promptly as the Bicslade one. Although under the original Act of June 1809 three years were given to complete a line up Howlers Slade, the estimates for its construction were not prepared

until December 1811. It was one mile in length and, rather than run along the valley floor, clung to a ledge on its northern side. Once again the branch was to serve quarries at the head of the valley together with some small coal workings *en route*. In the mid-1830s the Cannop Chemical Co. established its works alongside the tramroad at Cannop Bridge. This was the first of the 'steweries' established in the Forest and was followed by those at Oakwood and Tufts mentioned in Volume One. The works continued in use until about 1905 although the tramroad connection had been removed in 1901.

Another industry established alongside the Howlerslade line was a foundry set up by Trotter, Thomas & Co. The Cannop, or Howlers Slade, foundry was offering to supply tram plates to the S & W in 1836. The tramroad siding was removed in 1901 although the foundry continued in use until 1960.

As with the Bicslade branch, following the conversion of the main line tramroad to an edge railway the Howlerslade line was left as a feeder, terminating on the wharf at Cannop Siding. By about the First World War the tramroad was in use only for stone traffic, and with the recession in this industry after the war it fell into disuse about 1919/20. The tramplates remained *in situ* until recovery was sanctioned in September 1940, the removal taking place by January 1941. It is, however, possible that the section from the old Cannop Chemical works to Speech House Road may have survived a little longer to serve a Ministry of Supply saw mills which was set up close to the chemical works site during the Second World War.

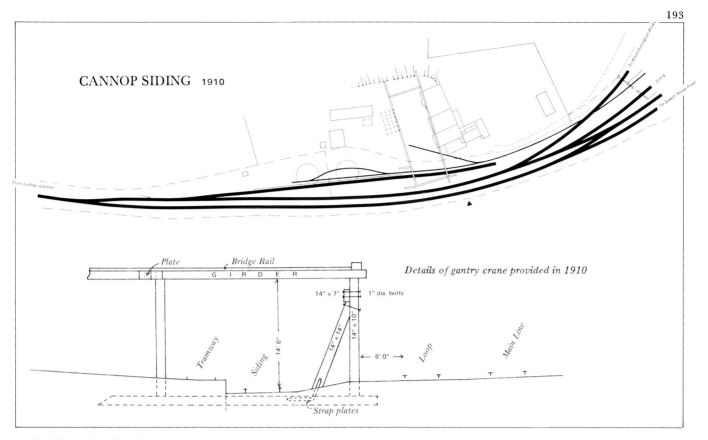

CANNOP SIDING 1910

Details of gantry crane provided in 1910

A rare glimpse of United Stone Firms works and the 1910 loading gantry straddling the extended Howlerslade wharf. This view, taken prior to 1914, shows the steam-powered gantry crane. The bracken in the wagon was used as cushioning for the cut stone blocks. The tripod crane in the foreground may well have been that provided in 1906 for **E. R. Payne.**

Gloucester Public Library

A short goods train signalled for the loop and entering Speech House Road on 25th July 1963.　　　*Keith Allford*

Another view of the same train alongside Cannop siding which served the disused Howlerslade wharf.　　　*Keith Allford*

The southernmost entry to the loop was controlled by the 2-lever 'Cannop Siding Ground Frame'. *Keith Allford*

A closer view of the ground frame. *Keith Allford*

WOOD DISTILLATION WORKS SIDING

To Coleford

Carpenters Shop

Wharf

S WAGONS

Offices

Charcoal

Boiler

Retort House

Wagon Turntable
Electric Capstan

Weighing Machine

Loaded wagons to gravitate from turntable and empties hauled back by wire rope and electric capstan.

To Howlerslade

TO WAGONS

Culvert

Engines not to proceed beyond this board

Station House

Goods Shed

Signal Box

Station Building

LOADING BANK

PLATFORM

TRAMWAY

HOWLERSLADE

Stone Saw Mills

14½ M.P.

Winberry Branch

To Serridge Junction

From Lydney Junction

0   1   2   3   4   5 CHAINS

An early view of the works about 1914 with the cylindrical retorts clearly visible in the foreground. Standing in front of them is one of the trucks, or cradles, which was filled with cordwood and pushed into the retorts.   *Public Records Office*

WOOD DISTILLATION WORKS

The works here began production in October 1913, being built and run by the Office of Woods. The idea behind them, first mooted in 1911, was to use the large quantities of waste wood generated during the felling of oak and other hardwoods. The Office of Woods could not finance the project alone, but help was on hand from the Government who, under the circumstances prevailing at the time, wished to make the best use of the country's natural resources, particularly in the case of such industries as wood distillation, some of whose products would be vital in the event of a war. The site chosen at Speech House Road was not only close to the railway but also to the junction of four roads, thereby aiding the movement of materials.

In April 1911 an application was submitted to the Joint Committee for a siding connection to the proposed works. The estimated cost, including a loop capable of holding ten wagons, was £1,011. This was evidently too much for the Office of Woods which, in July, submitted an alternative scheme for the provision of a tramway between the works

and Speech House Road station. This plan was approved in July 1912 and involved the diversion of the Joint Committee's cart road, the slewing of the Howlerslade tramroad (again), and the construction of a narrow gauge tramway which was to terminate in the station yard alongside the goods shed. At a site meeting the Crown's representative expressed the opinion that they could construct the tramway for less than the £95 estimated by the railway engineer, and this course of action was agreed upon subject to the works being completed to the satisfaction of the Committee's engineer. An agreement entered into between the two parties in November 1912 stipulated that the tramway within the station yard was not to interfere with vehicular access and also that if traffic to the works increased to such an extent that it interfered with the normal traffic to the siding, the Crown would have to construct their own independent siding. The work on the tramway was completed in April 1913.

The cost of the entire works was £15,000 with the plant being supplied, ironically, by F. H. Meyer of Hanover-Hainbolz in Germany. Technicians from that firm were responsible for the installation of the machinery within the

Another view, probably contemporary with that on the previous page, but looking in the opposite direction, showing some of the settling tanks, possibly the tar separator, on the right.
Collection Neil Parkhouse

buildings. At the time of construction only the production of charcoal, acetate of lime, wood spirit and wood tar was planned. It was intended eventually to produce acetone, used in the production of cordite, at the works but the First World War began before this could be done and the necessary retorts were not installed until 1915.

The wood used in the process was brought to the works from the surrounding forest by horses and mules. About 1,500 to 2,000 'cords' of timber were stacked in the works yard to provide a continuous supply during the winter when conditions often rendered the hauling of timber impossible. A 'cord' is a measure of 128 cubic feet of timber, and the wood used, known as 'cordwood', consisted mainly of branches. It was stacked about four feet wide and four feet high and every eight feet along the stack gave a cord.

The various processes within the works all began with the production of charcoal. Cordwood was taken from the stacking yard and loaded into a cradle which ran on standard gauge railway tracks. The cradles were cylindrical, about 6 feet in diameter and 10 feet in length, each holding approximately two cords (about 50-60 cwts of timber). The following description of the various processes is taken from a Government pamphlet on the works dated 1914:

'When ready the iron door of the retort is lifted and the trucks of wood are drawn in by an electric motor. [Five cradles made a 'charge' for the retort.] The door is then securely closed and the temperature raised to 330°-350°C. Distillation usually commences in about 2 hours and continues 20 to 22 hours.

'After the process is completed the door at the other end of the retort is raised, and the trucks, which now contain charcoal,

are quickly drawn by motor into an iron cooling-chamber similar in form to the retort. [The retort was a cylindrical iron box, 56 feet in length and 7' 6" in diameter.] The doors at each end of the cooling-chamber are made secure and the exterior is irrigated with water. The charge remained in the cooler for 24 hours after which it was removed and the charcoal was bagged up for sale. (To produce one ton of charcoal took about five tons of cordwood.)

'During the process of distillation about 70 per cent of the weight of the wood is given off in the form of gases, which pass out of the top of the retort through two copper pipes into a tar

A Marshall single cylinder horizontal steam engine used to power the works. It is seen when newly installed, probably in the late 1920s.
Collection John Roberts
courtesy Dean Heritage Museum Trust

Another view of the charcoal store, showing the bags of charcoal stacked inside. The gantry in the foreground is the lifting gear for the door on the end of the retort. *Keith Waters*

Another scene in September 1951 showing the traverser used to move the loaded cordwood cradles to the end of the retorts. *L. E. Copeland*

One of the rectangular retorts installed soon after the 1928 modernisation.   *Keith Waters*

separator, where the tar is condensed and flows into a tank. The tar is then run into a 'montejus' and lifted by a compressor into the tar still, where it is freed from the acid, oils and water remaining in it. It is run direct from the still into casks, and is then ready for marketing.

'The gases and vapours, freed from tar, pass out at the top of the separator, and on into a tubular condenser, where the naptha and acid vapours are condensed and run into large storage vats. This pyroligneous liquor, as it is called, is left in the vat three or four days to free it from any tar in suspension, and is then ready for further treatment.

'The incondensible gases pass from the tubular condenser into a gas washer, where any residual naptha or acid is removed by water, and are then conveyed by a pipe to the furnace, where they are utilised in the process of carbonation. [The furnace was situated underground to one side of the retort. It was coal fed and the hot gases were taken the full length of the retort by a flue and fed into it through port-holes.]

'The pyroligneous liquor, freed from tar, is pumped from the storage tanks across the yard to a vat in the acid room and neutralised with lime, which has been prepared in a lime mixing tank outside. The liquor is stirred continuously by a mechanical stirrer until the mixing and neutralisation are complete. Thence it is pumped into settling tanks at the top of the building, then into sludge tanks on the first floor, where further impurities are removed, and thence into a storage tank in the acid room.

'It is now pumped into a small 'clear liquor' tank on the top floor, and runs thence into the iron column of the continuous apparatus, where the neutralised acid liquor is completely separated from the naptha. The apparatus consists of a wrought-iron base or still, containing a copper coil, surmounted by a series of cast-iron plates. The neutralised liquor is run off continuously from the still into a tank below, and while still hot is pumped into an evaporating pan. It is there boiled down to a strength of ten degrees Baume, and when this point is reached, is run into the pan of a rotary drier. This is a large wrought-iron drum, heated internally with live steam. The drum revolves slowly in a shallow tank and picks up a coating of the neutralised liquor. The liquor is dried, as the drum revolves, to a content of about 70 per cent of grey acetate of lime, and then removed by a series of scrapers on the other side. The acetate, which is now in a pasty condition is spread upon a concrete drying floor, under which pass the gases from the retort to the chimney stack, and, after being dried for several hours is filled into sacks. The acetate now contains from 84 to 85 per cent of true acetate of lime.

'The naptha which runs from the top of the iron still and column, after being freed from the acetate of lime liquor as previously described and also from some of the heavy oils, is passed through a copper wash column, into which a weak solution of sulphuric acid trickles, and is here further purified. Thence it goes into a second column, where it is treated with a weak solution of caustic soda, and more oils are separated out. After passing through a small condenser the purified methyl alcohol is run into a storage tank below, and is ready for filling into drums for dispatch.'

With the commencement of hostilities in 1914 charcoal and acetate of lime became vital to the war effort and control of the works passed to the Ministry of Munitions of War. They paid the Office of Woods £16,000 for the buildings and plant and in September 1915 bought the site for £566. Various cottages at Cannop for housing workers at the plant were, however, retained by the Office of Woods.

Extension of the works was soon put in hand with the construction of the acetone retorts and the accompanying distilling plant. Two more retorts were also installed at this

The cordwood stacking ground with a couple of loaded cradles used in the retorts. These vehicles ran on standard gauge track and were moved around using electric haulage motors and capstans.   *Keith Waters*

time for the production of charcoal; these were smaller than the original and doubled the output.

To produce the acetone the acetate of lime was spread in shallow trays which were then stacked in cradles and placed into retorts. At a temperature of 450°-500°C acetone vapour was driven off and passed through a condenser and the resulting liquid was then distilled. The pure acetone was gained and treated with permanganate of potash whilst the 'acetone oils' also given off were used to produce camouflage 'dope'.

By 1917 traffic to and from the works had obviously increased as in January of that year it was reported that the provision of a siding, at the expense of the Ministry of Munitions, had been agreed upon. The submitted plans were approved provided that locomotives were not required to work beyond the 6 ft clearance at the entrance to the loop sidings. They merely had to place inwards wagons on one siding and remove outwards ones from the other. All movement of wagons within the works was carried out by capstans and electric winches. The sidings, estimated at £4,290, were reported as being completed in July 1918.

Production continued at 'H.M. Factory, Dean Forest' until May 1919 when it was closed down 'for the time being'. The Crown had been worried in March when it was rumoured that the buildings were to be sold to a firm of

'horse nail makers' and wanted an assurance that they would only be sold as a going concern as they were afraid that they would be unable to dispose of their cordwood! At this time about 2,500 cords were produced in Dean annually, approximately 500 being used for local household fires and 2,000 for the 'Distillery', which could consume 6,500 cords per year.

A closer view of one of the cradles.   *Keith Waters*

The wood distillation works was served by two sidings, that on the outside of the curve being used for the delivery of empties and that on the inside for loaded wagons awaiting collection after having passed over the weighbridge in the right foreground. Locomotives were not permitted past the stop board on the right which, curiously, according to plans was always positioned alongside the outward sidings and must have been frequently obscured. This picture, taken in the 1950s, shows only the remains of the severed inwards siding. It also serves to illustrate the unfenced station yard and private sidings of a pre-vandal age. The road on the left leads on to the Speech House.

R. Dagley-Morris

A '16XX' class pannier tank, No. 1627, on the wood distillation siding in April 1961. A culvert passing beneath the fenced opening to the right is spanned by two girders which may have supported the original tramway connecting the works to the station yard. *R. Dagley-Morris*

Two views of the works taken in 1973 after closure. The main portion of the works was built in red brick, this imposing structure dominating its surroundings.
Dr. D. V. Willetts

The works were advertised for sale in June 1919 with the 'Surplus Government Property Board, Factory Disposal Branch', promising to give the Crown due notice if they were to be sold for a purpose other than wood distillation. They remained empty until 1924 when they were taken over by Wood Distillation (England) Ltd., a private company who also took over the private siding agreement from 9th May.

The mid-1920s was not a good time for the industry with many small charcoal producers closing down. The Speech House works managed to keep going until 1927 when the new owners went into liquidation. They were bought the following year by Shirley Aldred & Co. Ltd., manufacturers of charcoal since 1796, but retained a separate identity.

Before the works were restarted they were completely modernised. Two rectangular retorts were bought second-hand and replaced the original cylindrical one, also new processes to improve the distilling were installed. These improvements gave higher yields and with the end of the economic slump in 1932 the company was ready to take a large share of the market.

During the Second World War very little maintenance was done and reconditioning of the plant was commenced immediately after the end of hostilities under the Deferred Repairs tax regulations. This rebuilding was completed in 1950 and in 1955 a solvent recovery plant was transferred to Speech House from Shirley-Aldred's works at Worksop. In 1960 the production of tar, acetate and wood spirit was discontinued, leaving just the manufacture of charcoal. This finally ceased when the works closed in June 1972, the siding agreement having been terminated in 1964 after the line from Coleford Junction to Speech House Road had closed the previous August.

Looking west over the wood distillation sidings with the weighbridge office featured alongside. *John Suckling*

No. 1639 near the stop board on the wood distillation sidings on 29th August 1960. Wagons were always propelled towards the works, which in latter years was generally served about twice a week. The traffic was mainly returned empty drums and, although the occasional 2-3 sheeted wagon loads of barrels were dispatched, most of the output was sent by road. *A. K. Pope*

As the yard and wood distillation siding were unfenced from the Coleford road, both sidings and the Howlerslade tramroad, which had been removed by this time, were gated. Whilst the running line continued through the station on a 1 in 165 gradient, steepening to 1 in 75 on the other side of the crossing, the goods siding fell away on a gentle down grade towards the buffers and the wood distillation siding curved away to the left on a steep embankment to the works. The difference in levels is apparent in this view taken on 24th September 1960.

R. Dagley-Morris

When the wood distillation siding was installed in 1918 it had to pass over the route of the already twice disturbed Howlerslade tramroad, and this picture, taken in August 1935, shows how this crossing was effected through the crude plateway. The later form of tramroad permanent way is seen here with cross timbers and lengths of Swindon rolled plates.

B. Baxter, courtesy R & CHS

'When after passing the great ponds upon the Cannop brook, we alight at Speech House Road station, the Forest meets us fairly in both senses of the word, exhibiting its beauties lavishly, yet scorning to conceal defects. Arrive upon an evening in late May or early June, and the ancestral hawthorns standing on the open stretch of turf beside the road are fragrant in the air . . . '

A. O. Cooke 1913

If any station can be said to have encapsulated the unique qualities of the Forest's railways, it was surely Speech House Road, arguably the most attractive on the S & W 'main line'. The setting was essentially rural, indeed the only dwelling in sight was the station master's house, and the meagre facilities were quite adequate for the few passengers using the station. The tranquil appearance, however, belied the station's status as a focus for the industrial traffic of the area, the enormous output from Cannop Colliery combining with the products of the Wood Distillation Works, Payne's Stone Works and several other local concerns to ensure that the peaceful atmosphere was frequently broken by the sound of locos at work. This view, looking north through the station in June 1922, has several points worthy of note. The station seats are unusual, being neither GWR nor Midland in origin, but possibly of local manufacture. The platform fence was originally of wooden 'space and pale' construction and ran from the front edge of the WC (see Volume 1, p. 24). This was later replaced by the 'unclimbable' fencing seen here, the portion nearest the WC being angled back to meet its rear edge. The timber structure on the left may have been erected to strengthen or supplement the yard crane, the jib of which can just be seen, and which was removed before 1939.

H. J. Patterson Rutherford

SPEECH HOUSE ROAD STATION

Speech House Road station, named after the famous Speech House nearby, began as a simple platform alongside the single line of the S & W, just north of Howlerslade siding which served as an interchange wharf for the Howlerslade tramroad. Although the line opened for passengers in 1875, it was not until November the following year that plans were submitted for a 'permanent station' and the extension of a siding alongside that serving Howlerslade wharf to form a loop so that mineral trains could be crossed or held clear of the main line. The new crossing loop and signals were controlled from two 5-lever open air ground frames, the arrangements being inspected and approved by the Board of Trade officer on 29th August 1878.

In the following November 'new connections at Speech House Road' were authorised. Details of these are not known but this may refer to the new crossover at the south end of the platform and the new siding to the north of the level crossing.

In 1888 a station master's house was built adjacent to the level crossing by James Hughes of Parkend for £190. By 6th August the following year, 'part of a new wharf and siding' had been constructed opposite the station, and on 23rd of the same month a small goods shed was ordered from Eassie's. Part of the Howlerslade tramroad had to be diverted away from the station in order to accommodate the new facilities. Again the progress of events is unclear but in November 1892, presumably following the commissioning of the new arrangements, the Board of Trade report mentions Speech House Road signals as being worked from an open frame on the platform with '8 levers, 1 spare'. The inspecting officer went on to recommend that the lever frame 'should be covered over and painted and maintained in a more serviceable condition than at present'.

A temporary siding for Messrs. Cruwys & Hobrough, contractors for the new road through the Forest, was completed in April 1903 for handling 'slag &c required in other works'. It appears that there was no formal agreement for the arrangement and the location of the siding remains a mystery, other than a vague clue from the *Dean Forest Mercury* for 23rd January 1903 in which there is mention that 'a cutting and siding are being put into Speech House Road station'.

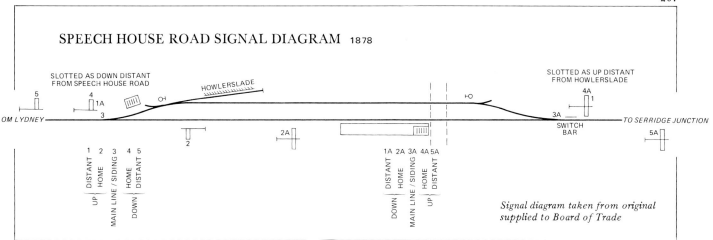

SPEECH HOUSE ROAD SIGNAL DIAGRAM 1878

SLOTTED AS DOWN DISTANT
FROM SPEECH HOUSE ROAD

HOWLERSLADE

SLOTTED AS UP DISTANT
FROM HOWLERSLADE

OM LYDNEY

TO SERRIDGE JUNCTION

SWITCH
BAR

UP { DISTANT HOME MAIN LINE / SIDING DOWN { HOME DISTANT

DOWN { DISTANT HOME MAIN LINE / SIDING UP { HOME DISTANT

*Signal diagram taken from original
supplied to Board of Trade*

Three years later, when the extensive Cannop colliery was being established alongside the Wimberry branch in 1906, it became evident that Speech House Road would become the centre of operations as far as the railway was concerned. Therefore, instead of merely replacing the existing signals which had become due for renewal, the opportunity was taken to adapt the layout for its new role.

The necessary revisions included complete resignalling and the provision of a new signal box, the work being authorised in September 1907 at an estimated cost of £830. The easing of a curve to the north of the station necessitated leasing extra land from the Crown and, in October 1909, an additional £121 was authorised for the resignalling.

In order to centralise operations, the old Wimberry Junction was abolished and the branch extended alongside the running line to connect with the existing crossing loop immediately north of the level crossing and close to the signal box. As this displaced a siding which had extended from the end of the loop, extra land was leased from the Crown and another was provided further north, clear of the new scissors crossover, becoming known as 'Woodbine' siding. The work involved in 'extending the Wimberry branch', estimated at a further £1,944, was authorised in April 1911 and completed in October 1912. However, it was not inspected by the Board of Trade until 4th March 1913. After this upheaval the station underwent few changes.

By the 1920s the staff complement at Speech House Road was as follows: 1 station master, class 5; 2 porters, class 2; and 2 signalmen, class 4. However, whilst the goods

The present Speech House, part of which dates from 1676, is built on the site of Kensley House. It was in the latter building that verderers' courts had been held since about 1335. The verderers looked after the vert and venison (vert; trees, undergrowth and herbage, venison; deer) in the Forest for the Crown. They held a 'court' every 40 days but its purpose was mainly administrative. As the local population appeared before the verderers to speak of their privileges the name 'speech house' gradually came into use. By 1858 the Speech House was being let by the Crown as an inn although it still contained the courtroom. The building was enlarged in 1883 and today is still a hotel, the courtroom doubling as a dining room.   *Collection Ian Pope*

The guard's view over the same train of empties featured previously at Coleford Junction, easing through Speech House Road while the fireman exchanges single line tokens with the signalman on 26th March 1948. The goods siding, which could hold 19 wagons, was used for general station traffic and machinery and supplies for Cannop and the wood distillation works. The 180 ft loading bank alongside was sometimes used to load Crown timber.   *L. E. Copeland*

This picture, showing the site of the approach of the re-routed Howlerslade tramroad in 1947, provides a good view of the otherwise neglected 20 ft Eassie goods shed adjacent to the Coleford road.   *L. E. Copeland*

The 'down' direction token catcher is apparent at the foot of the 260 ft platform in this c.1952 view looking south from the edge of the yard. *P. J. Garland*

receipts were increasing at this time in common with the rest of the system, the number of passengers booked from there had fallen from a mere 6,141 in 1925 to only 3,340 in 1927. The station was indeed remotely situated to the extent that passengers and staff alike, both here and at the equally isolated Drybrook Road, could hardly have been very surprised at the conquest of the enterprising bus companies.

After the withdrawal of passenger services in 1929 the station booking office and waiting room was retained for goods work, whilst the adjoining ladies room and WC was 'to be put out of use'. The gents' WC and urinal were kept for the convenience of the staff and the following items of equipment were recovered: table in signal box, 3 CI No. 2 lamp standards, 2 platform seats, 1 one-wheel barrow (another two-wheeled barrow was retained), 1 ticket dating

The site of the Howlerslade tramroad crossing over the wood distillation siding seen in 1939 after the removal of the tramroad. *L & GRP*

Despite the continuing efforts of PW gangs throughout the country, there are always problems in areas where sheep graze near the lineside. These all too readily dismissed, innocent-looking creatures have ways of finding any weakness in fencing and are inevitably found grazing on the inside of the boundary, much to the distress of loco crews. This picture, taken on 10th April 1960, shows one of the triumphant beasts surveying the scene from the platform.   *A. K. Pope*

The rather spartan urinal shows well in this view but the function of the adjoining cupboard/store has not been established. The fire buckets were provided following a Joint Committee decision in June 1906 to so equip all stations and signal boxes.   *P. J. Garland*

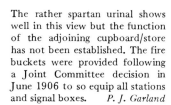

A number of the original 20 ft Eassie buildings were extended by the addition of another of similar size alongside, this particular one being added after 1894. The original is the nearer portion, whilst the join is accentuated by the uneven foundations which left the sections at different angles. Certain lighting improvements were authorised at Speech House Road in 1925 at a cost of £9, but the new lamps provided lasted only until the end of passenger services in 1929. The bracketed lamp in the foreground predates these short-lived improvements and originally had a twin adjacent to the WC (see page 206). Both were mounted on square wooden posts, an unusual feature which may date from Severn & Wye days.   *P. J. Garland*

The rear of the building showing not only the extent of the original structure but also the intermediate bridging section. The original chimneys on all the Eassie built S & W buildings were brick stacks angled at 45° to the main structure on one corner, each varying according to the local builder responsible.   *P. J. Garland*

machine, 1 ticket case. The three lamp standards and platform lamp cases, which had been provided only four years beforehand, were sent to Swindon on 8th November that year together with a lamp bracket and basket, an oil lamp, shade and ceiling protector, a framed and glazed fare table and three more oil lamps and glasses.

Although there were no longer any passenger trains calling at Speech House Road, the station nevertheless continued to bustle with the brisk goods activity. Traffic came into the yard for both the Wood Distillation works and Cannop Colliery. Several coal merchants had wagons brought in for local delivery of coal, one in particular remembered was T. D. Symonds.

The siding serving the goods shed was known as 'under the wall' or 'the hole' and was also used for the loading of Crown produce and undoubtedly coal from small concerns in the area.

Speech House Road saw a flurry of activity during the Second World War with ammunition being unloaded here. One Lydney driver well remembers the occasion on which he knocked a wagon into 'the hole' rather too hard considering its load of ammunition. Fearing the consequences he and his fireman cringed on the footplate! However, the feared explosion did not occur. Towards the end of 1942 'heavy traffic' was expected to arrive at Speech House Road.

After the war the station settled back to its normal tranquillity serving the needs of the local area.

The wooden post bracket starting signal 40/44. The left-hand arm (shorter than the main arm) read to the Wimberry branch. The main (i.e. higher) arm (44) was for the main line to Serridge Junction.

P. J. Garland

The c.1909 signal box and level crossing are the subject of the final picture selected from this photographer's visit c.1952. Arrangements for working the level crossing gates from the new signal box were proposed in October 1910, but it would appear that the work was never carried out. Following complaints received about delays to vehicular traffic at the crossing, it was decided in April 1911 to remove the box steps to the end of the cabin nearest the crossing 'so that the signalman may more promptly attend to the gates'. The replacement or repositioned steps formed an internal staircase, the position of the original entrance on the south end wall being obvious in the photo on page 214. The alterations cost £15.

P. J. Garland

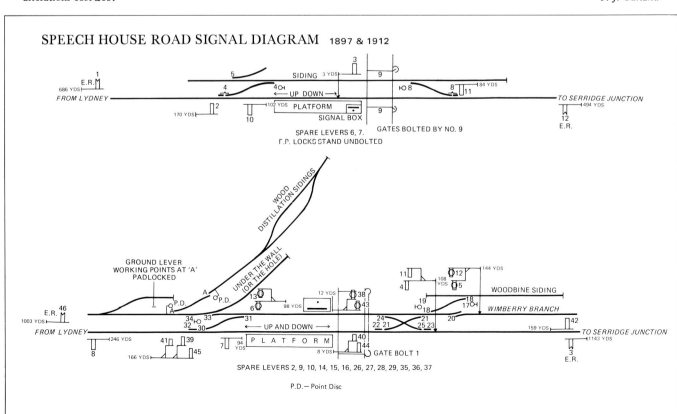

SPEECH HOUSE ROAD SIGNAL DIAGRAM   1897 & 1912

Linesman Mike Rees at work testing the lever frame, which was of a GWR design with 46 levers set at 5¼″ centres, with locking (below floor level) of the horizontal tappet 3-bar type. *Mike Rees*

Signalman Jack Baldwin resting in the sunlight filtering through the box windows. The box contained 46 levers of which 33 were in use. Speech House Road was one of the larger signal boxes on the S & W system, the locking room dimensions being 33′ 6″ x 12′ wide, with the operating floor 8 ft above rail level.

Keith Allford

No. 1632 alongside the signal box on 30th May 1960. In 1913 the Joint Committee proposed the provision of a lamp hut with tank and pump, but following a site visit it was decided that the requirement could be met by the conversion of the existing coal store (this could have been either inside the base of the box or the coal pen outside) into a petroleum store and the provision of a zinc-topped table in the signal box, the cost of the work being estimated at £11. However, whether in the event the corrugated iron hut alongside was provided instead of or in addition to the conversion is not clear. The wooden panelling in the end wall clearly shows the position of the original entrance and external staircase. The ringed bracket signal replaced its wooden post predecessor c.1950, the latter having been sited on the level crossing side of the signal box as shown on the signal diagram on page 212 and in the photograph on page 206.   *A. K. Pope*

The Forest of Dean was undeniably a railway backwater so it is perhaps not surprising that these S & T plates, generally out of use before 1914, should still be in evidence in 1960, albeit that they had probably been forgotten! Indeed even the changing of the colour of distant signal arms and lights from red to yellow did not take place on the S & W until April 1945! As this photograph was taken in the final years, the customary board walk over the emerging rods and wires at the base of the box was evidently not replaced but it does give an opportunity to see the mechanical arrangements normally hidden.

A. K. Pope

Looking south through the crossing in 1957.

Mike Rees

No doubt the older and stricter GWR hierarchy would have frowned upon such practice as catching the train token hoop by holding a broom out of the window, but this custom of later years saved the signalmen a great deal of running around. Here the fireman of No. 1627 is surrendering the token to signalman Jack Baldwin after his engine has been uncoupled from a recently arrived train on 1st August 1961.

A. K. Pope

The signalman's view of a train of empties being propelled along the Wimberry branch towards Cannop colliery in August 1960.

A. K. Pope

An unidentified pannier tank heading a southbound coal train over the level crossing in December 1960. The two bracket signals seen in this view were recent replacements which saw little use before closure north of Speech House Road.

Roy Denison

Despite the evidence of official records, it is almost certain that the level crossing gates were always hand-operated, as witnessed on this occasion on 26th March 1948. The station master's house, built in 1888, was from 1907 equipped with a tablet repeater bell to enable the station master to be called for duty after ordinary hours. The 'up' tablet/token catcher is featured in the foreground. *L. E. Copeland*

This scissors crossover providing access to the Wimberry branch and goods loop, was the showpiece of the 1910-12 layout revisions. The entrance to Woodbine siding is just visible immediately beyond the boarded foot crossing. *L. E. Copeland*

218

As if to amplify the point made on page 210, two more intrepid ovine explorers can be seen inspecting the permanent way gang's handiwork in this view looking south through the station in 1958. The station master's house with its well-tended garden is prominent on the right, the dwelling being occupied in later years by a PW ganger.
C. H. Townley

Looking north from the 'up' home signal (seen in the view below), with Woodbine Siding to the left, the Wimberry branch in the centre and the main line to Serridge on the right.   *Keith Allford*

A guard's view over a southbound train passing Speech House Road's replacement 'up' home signal in August 1960. The large sandbox prominent behind the brake handle was no luxury in the Forest.   *Keith Allford*

THE WIMBERRY BRANCH

The line into Wimberry Slade was originally a branch tramroad built to serve the Wimberry Colliery. It was completed at about the same time as the main line tramroad and was subsequently extended to serve other coal workings and quarries in the valley.

When the broad gauge was laid in 1868 it went as far as the Wimberry Colliery and took coal from there to the South Wales Railway, when the S & W's conversion to standard gauge became apparent in 1872. 'Mr. Thomas of Coleford' sent a letter dated 29th April pressing for narrow gauge accommodation to his colliery at 'Wimblow' and quarries at Howlerslade 'by which he anticipates increasing his output considerably'. In January 1874 Messrs. Trotter, Thomas & Co., the owners of the colliery, were authorised to extend the siding at 'Wimblow', probably because in the same month the abandonment of the tramroad was sanctioned, which meant that all traffic would have to be carried on the railway. The S & W agreed to 'lend the rails' and the applicants provided labour and carried out all necessary earthworks.

After the removal of the main line tramroad and part of the Wimberry branch, the upper portion continued to prosper and remained in use until 1939, traffic being transhipped onto the railway at a wharf latterly known as Hopewell Sidings.

Details of the broad gauge branch are unknown but it was probably little altered by the gauge conversion. The branch came off the main line on the 'down' side and was probably gated from an early date. A loop was shown just inside the gate on the 1877 S & W survey after which, on the curve taking the branch to the west, was a siding laid

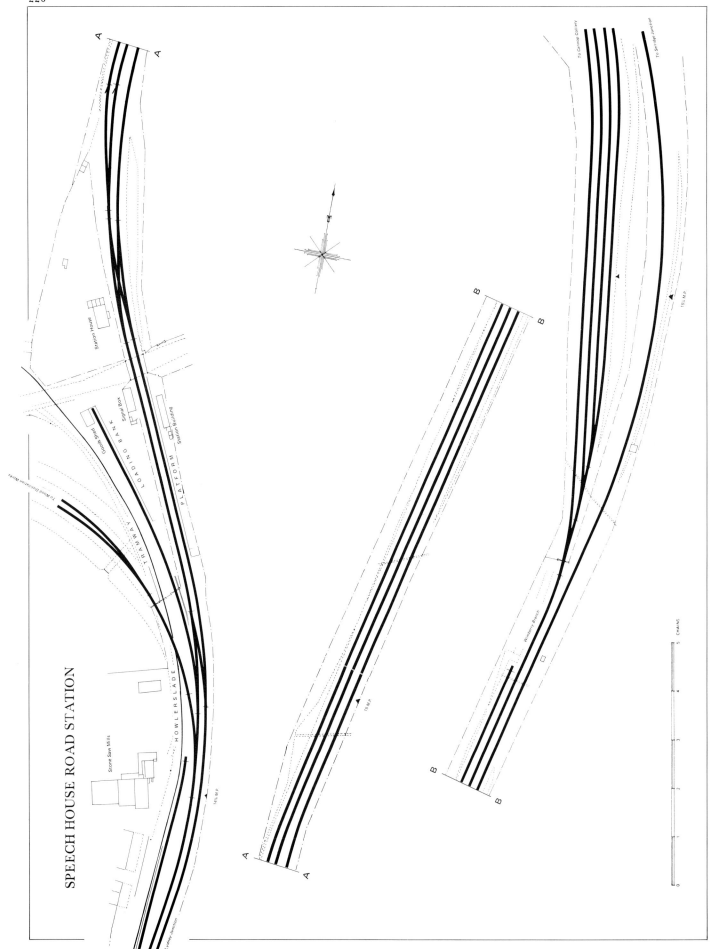

SPEECH HOUSE ROAD STATION

in 1874 for the convenience of the Wye Colliery Co. Strangely, although shown on the First Edition 25 inch and on the 1903 6 inch Ordnance Survey maps it is not marked on the S & W 1877 survey.

The Wye Colliery Co. were lessees of Speculation Colliery and had a pumping engine situated on the New Mill Engine gale. The history of Speculation Colliery will be dealt with in a subsequent volume, but a brief note about New Mill Engine is relevant here as it occurs later in connection with Speech House Hill Colliery and Cannop.

New Mill Engine was galed in February 1846 to a John Bannister on the site of the abandoned Old Mill Engine Colliery. It is likely that ownership had passed, at least in part, to Cornelius Brain in the 1850s and by 1873 it was being leased to the Wye Colliery Co.

In December 1875 they ceased pumping, both at Speculation and at the pumping engine here, known locally as 'Old Bobs'. Soon afterwards the workings of Trafalgar Colliery (see page 289) were flooded. This led to a law suit for damages against the Wye Colliery Co., the Trafalgar Co. contending that the cessation of pumping was responsible.

In April 1883 the Crown informed the Wye Colliery Co. that the time allowed them for opening the colliery was about to expire. Pumping was undoubtedly still being carried out on the gale but no coal was being won from it. Later in the same year the Wye Colliery Co. was dissolved when one of the partners, Richard Thomas, went into liquidation. (As mentioned in Volume 1, Thomas was the owner of Lydney tinplate works.) At the end of 1883 the gale was in the hands of the Trafalgar Colliery Co., which was owned by the Brain family, and in 1888 they sold it to the owners of the Speech House Hill Colliery.

The purpose of the short siding was to enable coal to be delivered to the pumping engine. Supplies were brought from Speculation Colliery, and in 1874 the proposed abandonment of the main line tramroad worried the Wye Colliery Co. as they had used this to link their two sites. The colliery company suggested two courses of action:-

1. To maintain the tramway either by buying the Severn & Wye plates or by laying their own
2. That a siding be put in 'near the pumping engine as this pumping engine is a source of permanent expense to us, we naturally wish to make the cheapest provision for the supply.'

The Severn & Wye replied that as the tramroad in question was crossed in two places by their new railway (the Mineral Loop from Tufts Junction to Wimberry) and knowing that it was to be abandoned, the bridges were of a temporary nature and were to be filled up. Option 2 was the best solution, especially as they had already laid in a siding near 'Old Bobs' at a cost of £100. For the carriage of coal from Speculation to the siding the Severn & Wye quoted a rate of 9d per ton. The Wye Colliery Co. objected to this, stating that it was only 3d per ton on the tramroad

This view shows the site of the original Wimberry Junction which was displaced when the branch was extended to Speech House Road.

Eric Parker

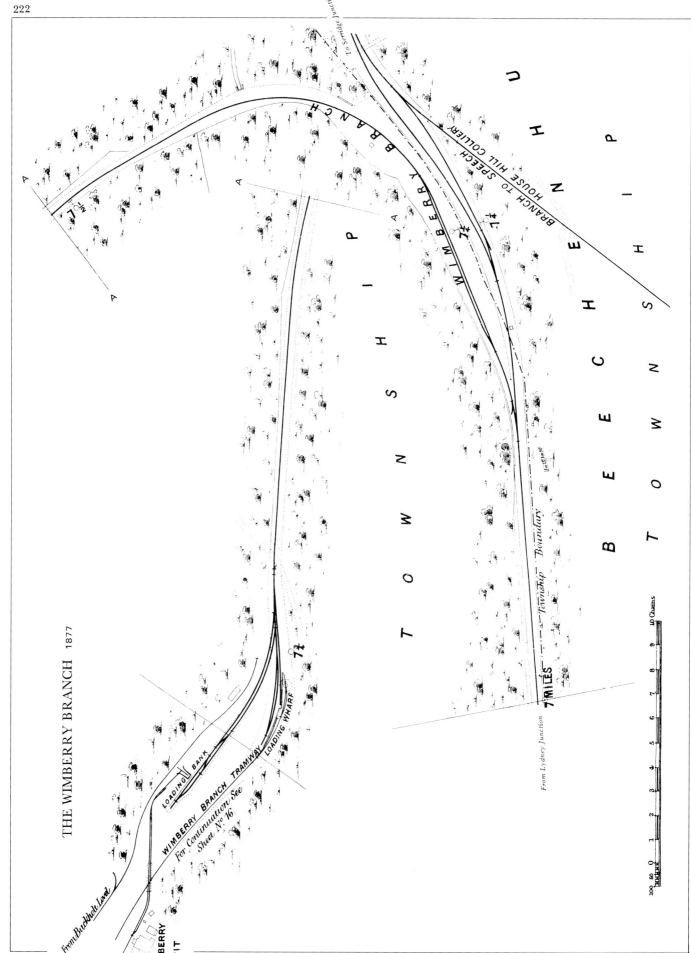

THE WIMBERRY BRANCH 1877

From Backhalt Lead

IMBERRY PIT

LOADING BANK

LOADING WHARF

WIMBERRY BRANCH TRAMWAY
For Continuation See
Sheet No. 16.

7¼

7 MILES

From Lydney Junction

Township Boundary

1 = 5⅛ m.a

7½

WIMBERRY BRANCH

BRANCH TO SPEECH HOUSE HILL COLLIERY

7¼
7¾

To Stridge Junction

A A
A A

TOWNSHIP

TOWNSHIP

BEECH HIP

BEECH TOWNS

100 50 0   1   2   3   4   5   6   7   8   9   10 Chains

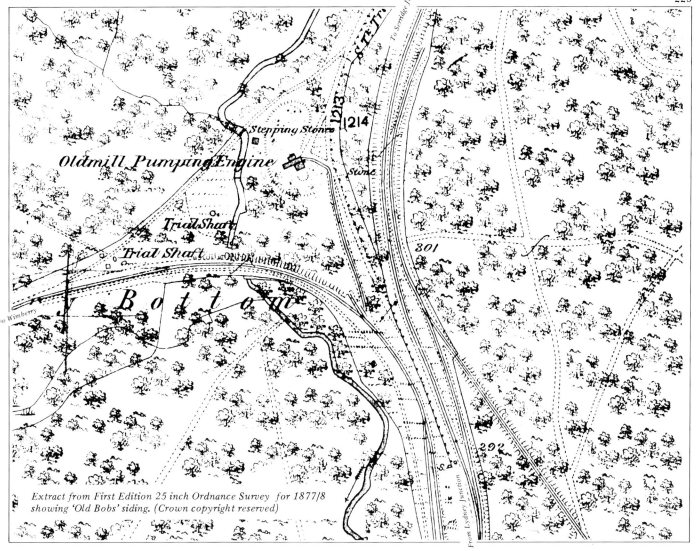

Extract from First Edition 25 inch Ordnance Survey for 1877/8 showing 'Old Bobs' siding. (Crown copyright reserved)

and asking if the railway would settle for 6d. It would appear that they were unsuccessful in this plea as, when in 1880 an application was made for a reduction in the rate for coal from Trafalgar Colliery to 'Old Bobs', from 11d to 9d, it was made on the grounds that '9d was the rate from Speculation and the distance was the same'.

The siding terminated about 60 yards from the pumping engine house, which brought further complaints from the Colliery Co. who wanted it taken to the house. The S & W, however, wished the Colliery Co. to complete the connection which, from cartographic evidence, would appear to have been achieved by laying a stretch of tramway.

Beyond the Wye Colliery Co's siding the branch continued in a virtually straight line to the interchange sidings. Over the years the only changes along this stretch, before the major upheaval caused by the construction of the adjacent Cannop Colliery after 1906, was the provision of a road underbridge in 1903/4.

Built in connection with the Crown's 'New Road', this bridge was not originally estimated for as the Crown anticipated that a level crossing would have sufficed at this point, especially as the line was only used for mineral traffic.

As at Coleford Junction, second-hand girders were used, the Joint Committee offering two 22 ft girders in December 1902 'at the cost of old iron'. This offer led the Crown to

see if the County Surveyor would allow them to construct the road sufficiently narrow to allow the use of the girders.

In early 1903 the contractors had estimated the cost of the bridge at £700, but the final design approved in June 1903 required an extra 3 ft headroom. To achieve this, the

This tranquil study looking south along the New Road towards Cannop shows the bridge provided in 1903/4.   *Keith Allford*

Looking back over the road underbridge in April 1961. The Wimberry branch is in the foreground. The far line is the independent connection put in to connect Cannop Colliery to its loaded wagon roads. In the middle distance is the pumping engine house on New Mill Engine gale, known locally as 'Old Bobs'.

R. Dagley-Morris

No. 1632, a '16XX' pannier tank, passing over the girder bridge which spanned the 'New Road', whose narrow width at this point was determined by the length of the second-hand girders available!

A. K. Pope

A rake of empty wagons standing on the Cannop loaded wagon siding just below the road underbridge with the Wimberry branch on the left. *Keith Allford*

No. 1625 propelling empty wagons into Cannop Colliery on 24th August 1955, having just passed over the points which gave access to the Cannop empty roads. *John Marshall*

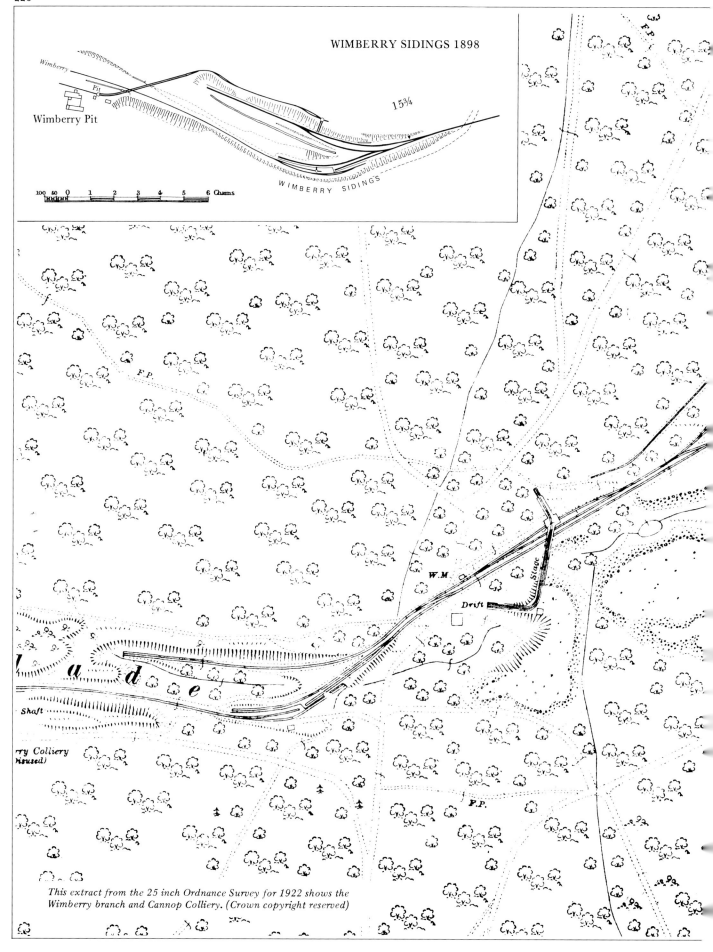

WIMBERRY SIDINGS 1898

Wimberry

Pit

Wimberry Pit

15¾

100 50 0 1 2 3 4 5 6 Chains

WIMBERRY SIDINGS

F.P.

F.P.

W.M.

Stage

Drift

l a d e

Shaft

rry Colliery
(disused)

F.P.

*This extract from the 25 inch Ordnance Survey for 1922 shows the
Wimberry branch and Cannop Colliery. (Crown copyright reserved)*

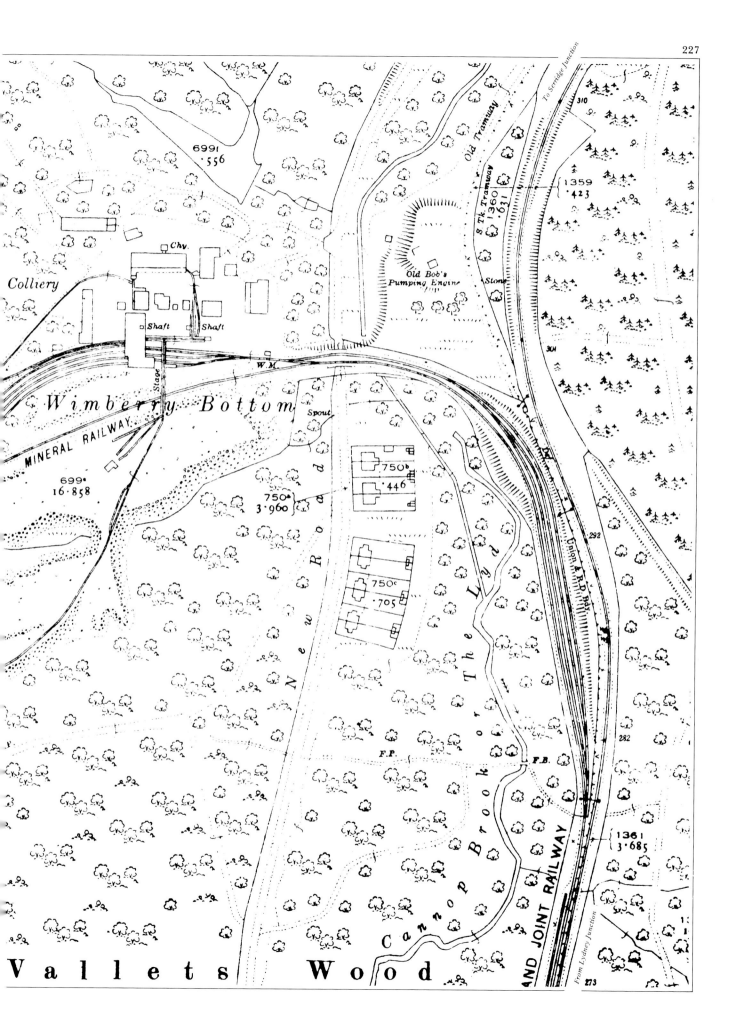

Colliery

6991
·556

Chy.

Shaft   Shaft

W.M.

Wimberry Bottom

MINERAL RAILWAY

Stage

Spout

699·
16·858

699·
16·858

750ᵇ
·446

750ᵃ
3·960

750ᶜ
·705

N e w   R o a d

Old Tramway

S.Tk. Tramway

1359
·423

1360
·621

310

304

Old Bob's
Pumping Engine

Stone

To Serridge Junction

292

Union & R.D. Rly.

282

The Lyd

F.P.

F.B.

C a n n o p   B r o o k

AND JOINT RAILWAY

1361
3·685

From Lydney Junction

273

V a l l e t s   W o o d

Looking back down the branch on 25th September 1960. The building on the left housed a haulage engine used for moving empty wagons around in the sidings, whilst in the distance it is just possible to see Cannop's empty wagon weighbridge built in 1938. The line on the right is the Wimberry branch itself, the loop on the left being used temporarily by Cannop Colliery in 1910. The point on the left, just beyond the engine house, once led to the screen road where coal from the Cannop drift was loaded from the overhead screens featured on the 25 inch Ordnance Survey map.   *R. Dagley-Morris*

formation of the Wimberry branch had to be raised at a cost, borne by the Crown, of approximately £150.

At the end of the ¾ mile branch were two sets of sidings. Those to the south serving the Wimberry tramroad interchange were probably laid in 1868, but details are very sketchy.

In 1874 Trotter, Thomas & Co. were given permission to extend the siding, and it may have been at this date that those to the north serving a loading bank for the tramway from Wimberry Colliery were added. The earliest plan is the 1877 survey reproduced here, but the 1898 survey shows that the accommodation had been cut back within both sets of sidings.

The commencement of Cannop Colliery also made for significant changes at this end of the branch. 'Temporary' sidings laid in by April 1907 may have included the long loop from which stemmed a further loop through a set of screens. These works are detailed under Cannop.

Following the closure of Wimberry Colliery it was agreed in January 1913 that the points leading to the siding should be removed. It would appear, however, that the siding itself was retained, now connected to the 1907 loop. It was into this siding that the empties were propelled for Cannop. Details of the workings into here, and Hopewell Sidings, are not recalled by the former drivers interviewed. They never

went right into them as they were always at the lower end of the long rakes of wagons being propelled!

Hopewell Sidings were disused by 1955, and probably well before that, the tramroad having been removed by 1946. In December 1955 the Chief Civil Engineer advised that they should be abandoned *in situ* as the sleepers had rotted completely and the whole site was overgrown. It was felt that the cost of recovery would outweigh the scrap value.

THE WIMBERRY TRAMROAD

The portion remaining after 1874, running up Wimberry Slade, served many coal mining and quarrying concerns. It ran for just over half a mile from the interchange through a secluded tree-lined valley.

The interchange probably got the name Hopewell Sidings from a number of small pits and levels served by the tramroad:- Hopewell, Upper Hopewell, Hopewell Level and Hopewell in Wimberry. At the head of the tramroad were quarries originally owned by E. R. Payne and Trotter, Thomas & Co. It has not been established when quarrying work ceased, but for a period the interchange wharf must have been busy with the transhipment of stone and coal.

Activity up and down the valley continued with many small coal works coming and going. This led to a succession of alterations to the tramroad over the years with new turn-outs and sidings being laid as late as 1928.

Traffic, however, only continued over the line for about another six years after this, a report in August 1939 stating that the line had been idle for some five years and that 14 chains had been removed, without authorisation, to repair the Bicslade branch. By June 1943 the remaining 38 chains had been wrecked by military tractors belonging to 131 Company, Royal Engineers, who were based at Coleford, working over the formation and pulling up the plates. Enquiries were made of any party who might still wish to use the line, but there seemed no prospect of it being used again and the remains were finally removed during 1946.

WIMBERRY COLLIERY

The Wimberry Colliery was situated on Old Furnace Level gale, originally granted to Aaron Hale and Edward Baldwin, both free miners, who assigned their interest on lease for 500 years to David Mushet in October 1821. The 1841 Award of Coal Mines, following Sopwith's survey, confirmed this. In 1847 David Mushet died and his interests passed to two of his sons, William and Robert. In 1855 they applied to the Crown for permission to sink a pit and establish a colliery at Old Furnace, but this was suspended the following year due to doubts about the position of the coal seam.

In 1864 the lease, possibly even ownership of the gale rights, passed to Trotter, Thomas & Co., the partners in which were John Trotter, Theophilus Trotter, James Thomas, William Whitworth, Nathan Atherton, Joseph Priestly and William Crowdry. This company evidently

began work at Wimberry as, in 1867, they wrote to the Severn & Wye stating that output from Wimberry Pit could be increased if it was served by a railway rather than a tram-road. As has been seen, they eventually gained this facility and in 1874 extended the siding, possibly adding the right-hand set of sidings featured on the 1877 plans.

By 1885, however, the company was in financial diffi-culties and the following year were unable to pay the dead rent due to the Crown. A report in 1890 shows that Old Furnace Level was disused and that the shafts were fenced round. In 1891 Old Furnace and another level held by the company, Vallets Level, were forfeited to the Crown for the non-payment of the dead rent.

In 1891 Old Furnace Level gale was regranted to a com-mittee of 160 free miners, headed by Benjamin Cooper, and they formed the Wimberry Colliery Co. A newspaper report about the new company explains why the colliery had previously failed. It states that flooding was the cause of closure and, as with both Cannop Colliery and Speech House Hill, water was always the greatest problem in this part of the coalfield.

The water problem came to a head at Wimberry in December 1897 when, on the 20th, a heading broke into some flooded old workings. Thirty-four men and boys managed to escape the influx and reach safety up the main shaft, but five men and a boy were cut off. The colliery manager, Mr. J. J. Joynes, immediately called for volunteers and with three others, Philip Watson, Samuel Mansfield and the under manager John Davies, went underground to effect a rescue. This was completed after 2 hours and for his part in it Joynes was awarded the Royal Humane

The mouth of the nearby Cannop drift, driven to enable coal to be worked while the new shafts were being sunk.   *L. E. Copeland*

'SHUTE' AT WIMBERRY FOR MILSOM HAMBLIN & SONS — AUGUST 1931

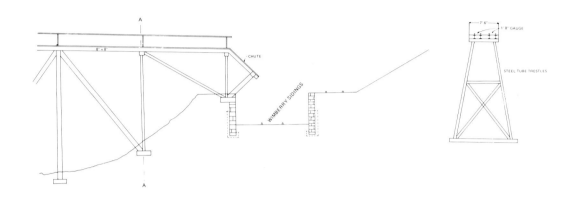

SCALE: 1mm to 1 foot

Hopewell sidings in 1935 with the Wimberry tramroad running along the wharf. The structure upon the wharf was a winch, believed to have been built by Samuel Hewlett of Soudley who cast the original S & W mileposts. The chute opposite the winch was provided in 1931 for loading coal, brought in trams from the workings of Milsom Hamblin & Sons at the Hopewell Drift Colliery.

B. Baxter, courtesy R & CHS

Looking round the curve of the old Wimberry Colliery siding. The sight of these two lines of rails overgrown and dappled by sunlight penetrating through the dense leafy canopy belies the use of them as a colliery headshunt. *R. Dagley-Morris*

Looking off the end of the tramroad interchange wharf at Wimberry with the old Wimberry Colliery siding, now in use as a headshunt for Cannop Colliery, going off on the left. *L. E. Copeland*

The end of the headshunt alongside the Wimberry Colliery loading bank seen in later years and heavily overgrown.   *A. K. Pope*

Society's silver medal, with bronze medals awarded to the other three.

In April 1900 it was reported that the workings in the Coleford High Delf seam had reached the barrier with Old Engine and Worral Hill Level gales. The owners of Wimberry asked permission from the Crown to work the coal in the barrier, having gained the consent of the owners of the adjacent gales. The Crown, however, refused permission for this. This meant that the colliery was virtually worked out, and the company started to work the 'pillars' back to pit bottom. Pillars were blocks of coal left in place to support the roof and prevent too much pressure being exerted on the underground roadways. Obviously once all the workable coal had been extracted the pillars could be removed, as supporting the roof was no longer of any consequence and the pillars provided quite a large amount of coal. As well as the problem of running out of workable coal, the company was also in financial trouble. In 1901 the debenture holders took control of the pit and were reported as endeavouring to dispose of it as a going concern.

From 8th July 1901 the colliery was leased to Amos W. Brown for a period of 5 years. He purchased all the colliery plant including the siding at the end of the Wimberry branch and the tramway linking it to the colliery. In 1904 it was discovered that a licence for the construction of the sidings and tramway had never been obtained from the Crown. One was promptly drawn up and signed, but only after Brown had attempted to gain the use of the siding for another of his interests further up the valley. The Crown, presumably still vexed about all the rent money they had lost over the years, promptly refused permission. In July 1904 Brown gave notice of his intention to cease pumping at Wimberry, but was informed that as he had not given notice to surrender the gale he must continue.

Following the 1904 Mines Act and the amalgamation of gales to enable the exploitation of the deeper coal measures, steps were being made to work this area of the coalfield. To this end a north country syndicate attempted to obtain Wimberry. The syndicate was led by a Mr. M. Maclean and

he offered £1,000, which was stated to be a fair price as the colliery was nearly worked out. The Wimberry Colliery Co., however, would not sell out, obviously thinking that they would gain a higher price, as the gale was wanted to save the sinking of new shafts which was an expensive business. It was said to the Crown that 'here was a wealthy gentleman ready to commence but stopped by a few miserable and stubborn people'. These were, of course, the 160 free miners, and it has to be said that £1,000 did not give each individual a very large return on his interest. By 1906, however, Maclean, as will be seen, had decided to sink new shafts elsewhere and thus the chance to sell Wimberry had gone.

In November 1907 the Wimberry Colliery Co. offered to sell out to Maclean and the Cannop Colliery Co. for £500, but all they were offered was £300! It is not clear whether the concern was still being worked at this time but the offer was finally accepted following a certain amount of pressure from the Crown, and in 1908 the Old Furnace gale was amalgamated into the Western United gale and became part of Cannop Colliery.

Unfortunately no photograph of the Wimberry Colliery has been discovered but here at least is a builder's photograph of a wagon supplied to the company in 1896.

Gloucester Railway Carriage & Wagon Co.

CANNOP COLLIERY

When, in early 1906, local newspapers carried the news that a north country syndicate had purchased two of the undeveloped deep gales, it began a period of local speculation. The two gales, Union & Cannop and Prince Albert, were bought from Messrs. Henry Crawshay & Co. who had acquired them, together with Speech House Hill Colliery, in 1903 (the history of Speech House Hill is dealt with later). The conjecture within the Forest was as to whether or not the syndicate were merely outside speculators or if they intended to develop the gales. It was hoped that the latter was the case in order to provide much needed employment following a long depression in the coal industry. When it was discovered that development was to proceed there was much local rejoicing, and fervent hopes were expressed for the prosperity and continuing success of the undertaking.

The syndicate was formed mainly of businessmen from Northumberland led by Mr. M. Maclean of Morwick Hall, Accrington. They formed the Cannop Coal Company Limited, which was registered on 28th June 1906 with a capital of £35,000 in 350 five per cent cumulative preference shares of £100 each.

Union & Cannop and Prince Albert gales were in the lower measures directly below the workings of Speech House Hill Colliery, which was working the upper measures.

It was the aim of the company to work the Coleford High Delf seam, the reserves in the two gales being estimated at between 10 and 12 million tons. To reach the coal new shafts were to be sunk on the Union & Cannop gale, and it was expected that the Coleford High Delf seam would be reached at a depth of about 200 yards. It was originally the syndicate's intention to use the Wimberry Colliery shafts, but they were unable to acquire the concern at that time.

J. J. Jones, late of the Wimberry and Speech House Hill Collieries, was appointed manager at Cannop, mainly due to his extensive local knowledge of the coalfield. It was he who prepared the plans for setting out the colliery, both above and below ground.

The colliery was set in a particularly attractive area of the Forest and when the layout of the necessary buildings was drawn up it was decided to preserve as much of the surroundings as possible. In order to erect the pithead buildings about 300 mature oaks had to be removed together with several tons of bracken. However, a large number of trees were to be left dotted around between the buildings and a belt of trees was also to hide the colliery from the Crown's new Parkend-Lydbrook road.

Work commenced on 10th July 1906 and by August the surface buildings had been started. On the western side of the site workshops were being built for blacksmiths, fitters

The view through the gate seen on page 221. The running line of the Wimberry branch is on the left, with the Cannop Colliery loaded wagon sidings on the right. Although primarily for the storage of loaded wagons, empties were sometimes left in these roads if the main 'empties sidings' further on into Wimberry Slade were full. They were later either propelled along the Wimberry branch if a locomotive was available, or pulled into the sidings by a stationary haulage engine situated just below the screens. Its rope would reach to 5 or 6 wagon lengths below the weighbridge but, to enable the sidings to be reached, an extra 50 yards long 'snatch' rope could be added. As already seen on page 228, a further haulage engine was situated beyond the empties sidings.

L. E. Copeland

234

CANNOP COLLIERY, FOREST OF DEAN

This aerial view of Cannop Colliery, taken in 1929, shows vehicles on the empty wagon siding, on the left, waiting to pass through the loading screens, over the weighbridge and into the loaded wagon sidings on the right. The new canteen and baths are visible to the right of the tall brick chimney whilst the small clearing in the trees further right was the location of the cleaning 'sprays'.

Courtesy I. J. Brown

An early view of the colliery, possibly circa 1910, while the sinking operations were still under way, the associated boilers and the chimney being visible on the extreme right. The chimney had a height of 100 feet and was built of local brick. The Wimberry branch in the foreground was laid with flat-bottomed rail, typical on the Severn & Wye, held to the sleepers by half a chair on the outside with a plate on the inside, both bolted through the sleeper.

Collection A. K. Pope

and joiners together with a saw-mills and a stores building. To the north work was well advanced on the siting of three Thompson 'egg ended' boilers, each 30 ft long and 8 ft 3 in in diameter with a working pressure of 100 p.s.i.

Just south of the colliery the Crown had agreed to erect two pairs of cottages and lease them to the colliery company. The plans for these were drawn up and shown to Maclean who immediately queried their size. They had been designed as 'substantial villas' with large gardens, but Maclean thought that he would have difficulty in letting them, stating 'that miners in the north would not be afforded such luxury accommodation'. The Crown declined his suggestion that smaller cottages should be built on the grounds that, since they would be alongside the new road, they could not be 'squalid small dwellings' but must be tidy housing as the road would be used by the majority of tourists entering the Forest. Another aspect of the architect's design queried by Maclean was the provision of a pig-sty in the garden. This doubt over the provision of another 'luxury' shows that Maclean was not as yet fully conversant with the Forest ways, as most colliers at this time kept pigs to supplement their income.

The underground workings of the colliery were to be laid out from two centre lines, one running north-south, the other due east-west. They were to be reached by two shafts 33 yards apart, each 14 ft in diameter, brick-lined and

surrounded by a 24 ft block of concrete to a depth of 4 ft. The purpose of the concrete around the shafts was to prevent 'creep', where the pressure of the surrounding strata forced the shaft out of line. This was particularly difficult to prevent where a lot of water was present, as in the case of Cannop.

To assist with the development of the colliery, the Crown, wishing to see the exploitation of the deep measures, loaned the sum of £20,000 which was primarily to be used in the sinking of the shafts. The loan was to be repaid in annual instalments once coal had been reached. The contract for the shaft sinking was let to Messrs. Moreman & Co. of Dunkerton, Somerset, and work commenced in July 1906. The Crown, anxious to keep an eye on their money, commissioned a series of quarterly reports on the sinking operation. These give an insight into the shaft sinking and the early life of the colliery once production had begun.

Preparations were also in hand to connect the colliery to the Wimberry branch. In April 1906 an application had been made to the Joint Committee for a temporary connection, which was approved on the proviso that the sidings were placed on the same side of the branch as the intended screens.

These temporary sidings were to serve a level, or 'drift', being driven to the Coleford High Delf seam slightly further up Wimberry Slade than the site of the new pits. The

Two views of the sinking operations. The upper photograph shows the temporary block and tackle arrangements used to lower materials and men down the shaft. This operation was performed using the 'kibble' or 'boick'. This was the bucket in which two of the men are standing and from which several were precipitated to their deaths during the sinking operations. The lower view shows a group of shaft sinkers which includes three young boys. Work on the shafts was probably almost complete at this time judging by the pipework going down the shaft and the cage shackles apparent behind the group.   *Collections A. K. Pope & I. J. Brown*

driving of this drift would enable coal to be put on the market before the shafts were finished, thereby generating some income for the company. This would assist the financing of the shafts and some of the coal produced could also be used in the company's boilers. The sidings, built at an estimated cost of £1,530, were reported complete, apart from a wagon weighbridge, in April 1907.

At the same time as the above siding arrangements were discussed, the layout of the permanent screens and sidings was decided upon. Sidings for loaded wagons were to be built between Wimberry Junction and the road underbridge on the branch. This meant that loaded wagons would pass over a short stretch of the Joint Committee's line and it was agreed, therefore, that the colliery company should be placed under an obligation to provide an independent line for the purpose when necessary. When this was finally done it meant the provision of a second span alongside the existing road underbridge. The cost of the empty wagon sidings and screen roads was estimated at £1,073, which did not include signalling or locking. The loaded wagon roads and the independent connection were estimated at £1,717 and the colliery company was to pay for each section as it was carried out.

Work on these sidings did not commence until coal was reached in the shafts. In April 1910 it was reported that traffic would commence in a few months and that it was therefore necessary for the work to proceed. The colliery company asked the Joint Committee if they would incur the outlay and allow them to pay the amount off with interest over five years, with the option of repayment at any time. This application was, however, declined by the Joint Committee which, at the same meeting, agreed that the colliery company could extend the screen roads on their own land and at their own expense in order to give more standing space for empty wagons. It was on this occasion that it was also decided that, to enable the prospective traffic to be worked satisfactorily, it would be necessary to carry out the contemplated extension of the Wimberry branch alongside the running line to a new junction at Speech House Road station, as already mentioned in the station description. It was explained that the colliery company wished to continue for the present using the run round at the end of the Wimberry branch as a screen line, and the Committee's consent to this arrangement was given as a temporary measure on the understanding that, when the pits were at work, the loop would be 'restored to the use for which it was constructed'.

Undeterred by their first refusal, in July the colliery company once again asked that the Joint Committee should expend the outlay, and again the request was rejected. However, a request to allow an alteration in the arrangement of the screen sidings to provide improved accommodation was granted.

In April 1911 the Cannop Coal Co. were again notified that the screen lines and loaded wagon sidings were required and that they should be proceeded with immediately. An amended plan was produced which showed the extension of the Wimberry branch to Speech House Road station. This had initially been proposed in April 1906 at a cost of £586; now however, a new siding, to replace one which would be displaced by the new line, was added to the plan, increasing the cost to £1,929. The expenditure was justified as the output from Cannop was soon expected to reach 1000 tons per day.

J. J. Joynes, the first manager of Cannop.

As well as notifying the colliery company that their sidings were necessary to operation, the Joint Committee also informed the Crown, who owned the land required. A memorandum in connection with this shows that the relationship between the colliery company and the railway was strained, as Mr. Joynes of the Cannop Coal Co. told the Deputy Surveyor 'that his Company don't want their hands forced' over the sidings and that they 'don't want any work to begin for three months'. The Joint Committee did not, in fact, take possession of the land until November 1911.

The first of the Crown's quarterly reports of the sinking operations was produced on 19th October 1908 and shows that both shafts had been sunk to a depth of 125 yards. The number 2 shaft, which was to be the pumping shaft, was walled to that depth and the number 1 shaft, the main winding shaft, was in the process of being walled. To keep them free from water electrical pumping plant had been installed, comprising two Bellis & Morcon engines driving two dynamos which in turn powered a turbine pump capable of lifting 2,000 gallons per minute.

The drift, driven at a point midway between the Wimberry Colliery and the Cannop pits, had, by 19th October, reached the Coleford High Delf seam, which proved to be 5 feet thick. A temporary electric pump, capable of handling 500 gallons a minute, had been installed and the equipment necessary to haul the coal out of the drift had been ordered. It was intended that an output of between 200 and 300 tons per day should be obtained until the pits were completed. The screening arrangements over the sidings were also well in hand, it being planned that empty wagons should be placed into the sidings at the western connection off the Wimberry branch and loaded ones removed at the eastern end.

By the end of January 1909 No. 2 shaft had reached a depth of 155 yards and No. 1 was down to 142 yards, with 2,500 gallons of water being pumped from them every minute. In the drift the main 'dipple', or roadway, was 70 yards into the coal. It was found that the seam was of consistent quality and that the roof above was good. A pair of levels had been driven off the main dipple and the haulage arrangements were approaching completion. It was hoped that the first truck of coal from the drift would be dispatched in February.

A newspaper report of February 1909 shows what a hazardous job shaft sinking could be. A young man was killed when the tub in which he was being brought up the shaft turned over and he fell 150 feet to his death. The following month the accident was repeated and another young man was precipitated to his death. In early May the electric pumps in the shafts broke down and, although they were soon repaired, the steam pumps were also overcome and the shafts were flooded. The Crown's May report shows that No. 1 was down to 165 yards and No. 2 to 167 yards. The main dipple in the drift had been pushed on a further 60 yards and both the levels were in good coal The output of the drift was around 150 tons per day and by September

it had reached 230 tons. At this time No. 1 shaft was down 192 yards and the depth in No. 2 was 183 yards.

On 25th November 1909 the Coleford High Delf seam was struck in the No. 1, or Deep Pit, at a depth of 204 yards. The shaft was then sunk a further 4 yards and the coal proved to be 4′ 9″ thick. No. 1 was known as the Deep Pit as it was on the side where the coal measures dipped deeper, whilst the other shaft on the upper side, where the coal was rising towards the surface, was called the Land Pit. No. 2 shaft at 203 yards was also into the coal by January 1910, when they were pumping 2,200 gallons per minute on average. The drift at this time had been driven 187 yards and three levels went off to the north and three to the south. Production, however, was still around 230 tons per day due to a problem with water.

The pits were flooded again in April after the pumps had broken down once more, but the water problem in the drift had been overcome and output had risen to 250 tons per day. By October the shafts were again dry and the first of the permanent steam driven pumps was being installed at pit bottom. It was located in a room built off a heading which had been driven to unite the two shafts, and where it was intended that two pumps would be situated. In another room across the heading two electrically powered pumps were to be placed. The output from the drift in

A similar viewpoint to that on page 235 but with the colliery now in production, as witnessed by the loaded wagon emerging from the screens. Coal was sold for local consumption from the land sales wharf in front of the wagon. The timber staging above brought tubs directly to the wharf from the pit-head. At its end can be seen a rotary tippler to invert the tubs and deliver the coal to the wharf below. The horse and cart on the right was probably collecting coal from the wharf. A weighbridge was situated just inside the colliery gates to weigh the land sales traffic.

Collection A. K. Pope

An early view of the screens looking north. The timber trestle bridge was provided in 1907 to convey waste material from the pits to the dirt tip.

Collection N. Parkhouse

October had further increased to a total of 350 tons per day, of which 60 were consumed in the boilers at the pithead.

Further water problems were encountered in December 1910 when both the pits and the drift were inundated, and they were not completely drained until February 1911. By May of that year a heading had been driven a distance of 35 yards from the bottom of No. 2 shaft. Production in the drift was shown to have increased to 440 tons per day, the figures for the previous two months being 8,547 tons in March and 10,148 tons in April.

The heading from the bottom of No. 2 shaft not only encountered water problems, which were to bedevil Cannop throughout its life, but also met some minor geological difficulties. In an endeavour to reduce the flow of water into the workings, trials were carried out to find out where it was coming from. It was found that by improving the surface drainage in some areas, several miles from the colliery, and by stopping the passage of water down swallow holes, the amount of water pumped dropped, especially during wet periods. Several stream beds around the colliery were concreted over in an attempt to stop seepage through the ground, and again this made a difference to the volume of water pumped.

Ironically, despite the constant ingress below the surface, the only source of fresh water at Cannop for the colliers to fill their water bottles was a spring contained in a small hut just inside the colliery entrance off the New Road.

By November 1911, two compressed air coal cutting machines had been installed and were working in the pits. The drift was producing 420 tons per day, the lower total being due to a strike in September and a lock-out in

October, from which production was just recovering. The reason for the strike was the employment of 17 non-unionists and the lock-out of 400 workmen was brought about when the men refused to discharge their 'check-weighman'. The position of checkweighman was extremely important as it was his job to weigh all the tubs of coal brought to the surface and record the weight against the team of colliers who had filled the tub, (on to which was chalked their mark) thereby determining their wages. He also checked the tubs to make sure that they were not partially filled with rock or other waste materials. A check-weighman had therefore to be someone whom the men trusted, and he was elected to the position by the work-force.

On the surface the erection of the screening plant, capable of handling 1,000 tons of coal in 16 hours, to take the output from the pits had commenced and these were virtually ready for use in February 1912. In April that year No. 1 shaft was being fitted out with its cages and their rope guides ready to commence winding coal. All the temporary sinking plant had been removed from the shaft and the opportunity was being taken to overhaul the winding engine. In August 1912, 380 tons per day were being brought up the shaft and, in November, the peak output of the year was reached when the combined total from the drift and the pits was 880 tons in one day. It was also around this time that work commenced on the colliery's office block, for which extra land was leased from the Crown. The building was to be of brick with a red tiled roof and to cost around £1,000 and, once again, in an attempt to blend it into the surroundings, it was decided to surround the offices with ornamental trees and shrubs.

240

A selection of Cannop wagons all built by the Gloucester Railway Carriage & Wagon Co.   *GRC & W Co.*

With coal now being produced from the pits, six years after sinking commenced, the Crown became less interested in the proceedings at Cannop. They were happy in that their loan was being repaid and decided to dispense with the quarterly reports, but until all the money had been repaid they kept up periodical surveys, commencing in October 1913.

This report gives the output from the pits as 580 tons per day. There was no coal being produced from the drift as once again water had broken in and flooded the workings, although by this time it had been de-watered and the roadways had been recovered. An attempt was made to drain the water from the coal on the west side of the drift by re-opening the Furnace Level, but this met with considerable difficulty and was abandoned. By January 1914 the drift was again in production, 250 tons a day being produced. This figure remained reasonably constant until March 1915 when it was decided to run down the drift and concentrate production at the pits, whose output at this time was averaging 1,000 tons per day.

By July 1915, however, the output had declined to 650 tons due to men being called to the colours and the ensuing shortage of labour. Work on closing down the drift continued, with the pillars of coal left as roof supports being worked back towards the mouth of the drift. Work finally stopped here in February 1916 and all men employed in the drift were transferred to the pits. By April 1916 the workings on the north and north-western sides of the main colliery had reached the boundary of the gale and so pillaring was also going on here. Throughout 1916 the average output was 750 tons per day.

An accident occurred during July 1917 when four men involved in the pillaring operation were caught by a roof fall. Luckily two of them were on the safe side of the fall and escaped injury. The other two, however, who were brothers by the names of Thomas and James Burnett, were trapped. Thomas was trapped by his legs on the surface side of the fall, but James was cut off. All the colliery officials were summoned to the scene, together with a doctor, and after two hours Thomas was released unhurt. During this period a conversation was held with James and work subsequently commenced to extricate him. The rescuers did not want to clear the fall in case it brought more of the roof down and so it was decided to dig a road out in the coal around the fall. Four and a half yards were dug out by pick in four hours and James was brought out after 6½ hours imprisonment. One of his first remarks was reported as being 'That's the first time I've ever had to be dug out.' The withdrawal of pillars was completed in this area in early 1918.

In 1917 the Cannop Colliery Company acquired the New Mill Engine gale from a Mr. W. D. Meredith. The gale was previously part of Speech House Hill Colliery and had been surrendered to the Crown in 1905 by Henry Crawshay & Co. Mr. Meredith had applied for a re-grant of the gale in October 1916 and it was acquired by Cannop in order to consolidate their area. Also in 1917 an application was made to the Crown for an extension of tip space. The spoil from the colliery was tipped to the south of the site, on the opposite side of the Wimberry branch, in an area of marshy ground. The original Crown licence for tip space stated that the height of the tip was not to go above the 'level of the passenger line from Speech House Road to Cinderford.'

The colliery continued through the 1920s with increasing production until a figure of 1,400 to at least 1,500 tons per day was reached by the workforce of about 1,040 men and boys. An official report stated there was accommodation for approximately 150 empty wagons at Cannop, the daily output from which exceeded this capacity. The increased output from this and other Forest collieries placed a strain on the Joint Committee, who were unable to find sufficient storage space for the empty wagons and often had to put a stop on the flow of all empties to the S & W. Consequently, at a meeting in February 1929, it was decided to increase the siding space at Cannop. At this time the sidings were usually cleared three times a day but, owing to the gradient on which they were situated, only 15 empties could be propelled in at a time. This apparently meant eight trips from the colliery gate to the empty wagon sidings, and even in good weather this was a difficult task for the best of drivers. According to a report, on the first trip to Cannop the empties were left, and loaded wagons

collected from the sidings just inside the gate, but these sidings were usually so full that the balance of empties was stored on Woodbine siding until later in the day. As the Joint Committee obviously felt that Woodbine siding had became vital to colliery traffic, it decided to require the Coal Company to lease it for £60 per annum under a private siding agreement of 22nd October 1930. Therefore it seems the desire for 'increased' siding space was simply met by making the colliery pay for the privilege of using the existing arrangements (works which they had financed). Furthermore the agreement allowed the GW and LMS to continue to use it for stabling empty 'Macaws' and 'Mites' for timber traffic loading at Speech House Road, where the yard accommodation was very limited, 'but not to the prejudice of the Licensees' traffic'!

It was subsequently used as an overflow for loaded wagons, especially when the colliery was 'at a stand'. If the loaded wagon road was full and there was nowhere to put the loaded wagons, which in turn meant that no more

In July 1915, in an attempt to combat the water problem at Cannop, two new boilers were ordered to provide power for extra steam pumping plant. There was some doubt amongst the management that the equipment would be readily forthcoming, as industrial production was being concentrated on the war effort. Cannop itself was not directly involved, as it supplied no coal to the Government, and attempts were made to get the Office of Woods to pull some strings in Governmental circles. These overtures were met with polite rejection so the colliery manager, J. J. Joynes, was sent to visit all companies supplied with coal by Cannop to see if any would be hampered in producing vital parts for the war effort if Cannop coal were not available. It was proposed to use this as a lever to get the new boilers. These efforts were, however, unnecessary as the new plant arrived quicker than expected! This view shows one of the new boilers being installed in September 1915. *Collection A. K. Pope*

A general view of the colliery, looking north from the dirt-tip in 1929, with the new baths and canteen under construction in the background.
E. Runicles, courtesy F. Webb

trucks could be filled at the screens, the colliery came to a stop. When this occurred the weighman at the colliery would telephone Speech House Road to request a clearance. The next available locomotive would then be despatched to move wagons out of the loaded sidings and into 'Woodbine', where they would be kept until a train was made up. Trains would also be made up in 'Woodbine' if there were too

many wagons to be pulled out of the colliery in one go, wagons being put into the siding in two or three lots.

The next major change to the appearance of the surface buildings was the construction of the canteen and pit-head baths in 1929. Before construction began a ballot was taken amongst the men as to whether the facilities were required. This showed that most men were in favour, and in fact a

continued on page 260

Two further views of the construction of the baths and canteen provided 'for the comfort of the miners'.   *E. Runicles, courtesy F. Webb*

Another photograph taken from the dirt-tip, this time showing more detail of the tramway scaling it. The Wimberry branch can be seen at the foot of the tip running under two steel and concrete bridges provided in 1926, replacing the timber trestle seen on page 239. The bridge on the right carried tubs full of dirt to the tip and the one nearest the camera returned the empties to the pit-head. In fact a rake, or 'journey', of empty tubs can be seen on the bridge. The colliery offices can be seen through the trees to the right of the furthermost head-frame. They were surmounted by a clock which could be seen from all corners of the colliery yard and was illuminated at night. Apparently it always showed the 'right' time!

E. Runicles, courtesy F. Webb

Looking from the top of one of the headframes at the huge 'new' dirt-tip which dwarfed the original or 'old' tip behind. During the Second World War the tip caught fire. This is thought to have resulted from hot boiler ashes being tipped, many millions of gallons of water being sprayed onto the tip in an attempt to extinguish it, but even so it burned for several years. After this occurrence all ashes were damped down before being tipped.

E. Runicles, courtesy F. Webb

Here we have more details of the tramway ascending the dirt-tip. At the bottom of the incline the tubs of dirt were loaded onto wheeled platforms or 'jacks' which kept the tub horizontal on its trip up the tip. They were hauled up on an endless rope powered by a 50 hp haulage engine. At the top the tubs were tipped automatically from girders extending out over the end of the tip. As this operation continued 24 hours a day the girders had to be extended quite frequently, with two men climbing to the top to carry this out. They also had to climb the incline if anything occurred to stop the tubs being tipped. This was an arduous task, particularly at night as the tip was unlit and its sides very steep.

E. Runicles, courtesy F. Webb

A closer view of the base of the tramway up the dirt-tip with the 'jacks' at the bottom. Beyond the crude shelter are 'journeys' of drams full of spoil awaiting tipping.

L. E. Copeland

Another aerial view of the colliery, looking northwards, probably in the mid-1930s. The full enormity of the dirt-tip can be seen together with the layout of the empty wagon sidings.

Courtesy John Belcher

The pneumatic dry cleaning plant installed around 1930/31 is featured on the left of this scene. This enabled the very small coal and coal dust to be separated from the dirt and shale. The small coal and dirt from the screens was taken up the angled conveyor to the top of the building where it was deposited onto shaker tables, the small coal passing off one end and the shale and dust off the other. The small coal then either passed into hoppers for loading into wagons beneath, or was taken by conveyor to the colliery's boilers. The shale and dust from the tables was taken to the conical structure which housed silk cones some 22 ft high by 2 ft wide. Here the fine coal dust was sucked into the vertical cones where it was held in suspension while the dirt was removed from below. The dirt was taken away by the long conveyor on the right-hand side and deposited into the hopper above the dirt bridge. When this required emptying a 'journey' of empty tubs was drawn underneath, loaded, and taken away to the tip. Once the dirt was out of the way, the coal dust was allowed to fall into a hopper and loaded into steel wagons and sheeted over for dispatch. Coal dust was used in many products including paint, black lead and compressed coal briquettes. The plant was fully automatic and was controlled from a central panel with each section of the process switching on in turn.

Courtesy I. J. Brown

Plan of the bridge in the foreground of the above photograph

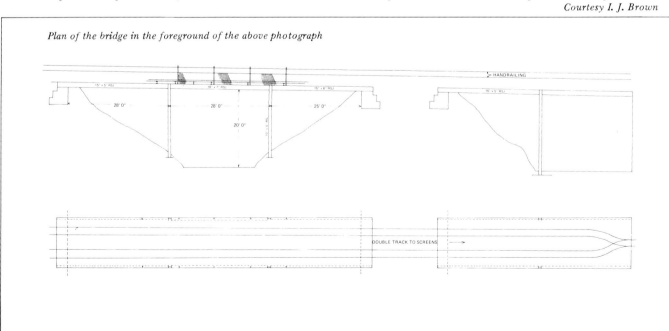

Looking over the top of the boilers in the colliery yard showing the main steam pipes coming from them. The expansion loop in the pipe in the foreground was always a favourite spot to sit in cold weather!   *E. Runicles, courtesy F. Webb*

A view along the impressive row of ten boilers, nine of which were in use at any one time while one was being washed out. The boiler nearest the camera was the No. 1 boiler with the leading stoker standing alongside. All nine boilers were worked as one, and if the leading stoker picked up his shovel to fire, then the others followed. The same went for feed water and even raking the fires through.

E. Runicles, courtesy F. Webb

The main steam winding engine.   *E. Runicles, courtesy F. Webb*

Part of the generating set with the main switchboard behind. *Collection A. K. Pope*

The mains electric generating set built by British Thompson Houston Co. Ltd. of Rugby.
Courtesy I. J. Brown

The top, or 'bank', of No. 1 pit, the main coal winding shaft. As can be seen, there were two cages in the shaft, and the gates across the top were lifted automatically when the cage reached the top. When in use for coal winding, the gates were fixed in the 'up' position to speed the operation. Men were wound up and down at about 17 ft per second but tubs were put up and down considerably faster, about 32 ft per second.

E. Runicles, courtesy F. Webb

We begin the following underground sequence with two colliers working at their allotted section of the coal face with picks and shovels. The rails in the foreground enabled a coal tub or 'dram' to be run up to the face for filling. Notice also, just above the handle of the spade, the candle stuck in the wall to give some flickering illumination. Working at the seam like this was dangerous as work was being done ahead of any timbering and the roof was liable to come down as the coal was removed. *Collection J. James*

Colliers resting at the coal face, savouring their bread and cheese and cold tea. The metal sandwich boxes were necessary underground, as any other material would soon be chewed through by the rats. As in the previous view, a candle can be seen on the right. *Collection J. James*

Horses were used for moving the drams from the coal faces to the main haulage roads. The harness arrangement, to which the haulage chain is attached, known as a 'jinny', would be worn throughout the shift. The open ventilation doors, visible either side of the horse, allowed movement of air through the underground workings. *Collection J. James*

Once the drams had reached a main roadway they were made up into 'journeys' of anything from 15 to 30 drams coupled together. Here a haulage rope is being attached to the leading dram.
Collection J. James

A further view of the same journey which, having been drawn forward by the haulage engine, is having the tail rope attached. Haulage with head and tail ropes enabled the journey to be moved forwards and backwards at will.
Collection J. James

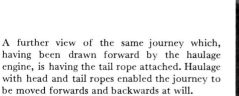

A journey coming over the top of a 'dipple' or slope *en route* to pit bottom.

Collection J. James

One of the underground haulage engines. These varied in size from small ones close to the coal faces to large ones at pit bottom. The larger, more powerful engines could haul 30 drams over a mile at 10-15 mph.

Collection J. James

Top & Above left: Two views of one of the underground electric haulage engines used for raising and lowering the 'journeys' of tubs up and down the inclines, or 'slopes'. The engine room was hewn out of the rock above the main roadway, the tubs passing beneath. *Above right:* One of the trolleys used to transport the colliers up and down the underground inclines.

E. Runicles, courtesy F. Webb

Pit bottom with a couple of loaded drams being pushed into the cage by the 'on-setter'. Pit bottom was the busiest part of the pit underground, with loaded drams constantly arriving at one side and empties being pushed off at the other.

Collection J. James

One of the sets of underground electric pumps situated in the roadway between the bottoms of the two shafts.　　*Collection J. James*

Closer to the coal face, water was channelled in pipes before being pumped to the surface by the plant seen in the previous view.

Collection J. James

Changing the pit ponies at the end of a shift. Unlike some collieries where they never saw the light of day throughout their working lives, those at Cannop were brought up and stabled on the surface, being raised and lowered in a specially constructed box. Twelve ponies could be brought up and twelve sent down in 20 minutes.

E. Runicles, courtesy F. Webb

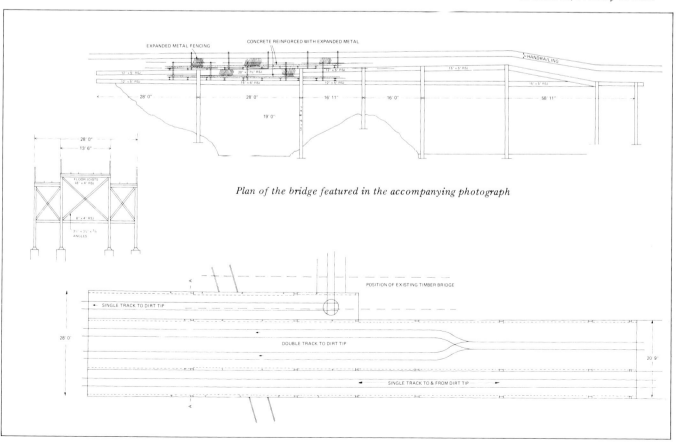

Plan of the bridge featured in the accompanying photograph

Three views of pit ponies at Cannop. The white pony on the left is believed to have been named 'Tinker'. *E. Runicles, courtesy F. Webb*

One of the ponies being clipped using hand-powered clippers. These animals were always extremely well looked after and any man found mistreating them would find himself in serious trouble.

E. Runicles, courtesy F. Webb

A group of Cannop workers.

E. Runicles, courtesy F. Webb

Another Cannop wagon, this time photographed at the colliery.

L. E. Copeland

The road entrance to the colliery viewed from the railway embankment.   *E. Runicles, courtesy F. Webb*

A fine selection of 'buses waiting to take men home at the end of a shift. They always waited in the same order; those for Coleford are nearest the camera, for Cinderford in the middle, and for Lydbrook at the far end. The lay-by was provided in 1930/31 by the colliery company. At first the County Council was approached to provide the facility but they declined to do so, fearing that they might set a precedent for every industrial concern in the county!

Collection A. K. Pope

Repairs of all kinds were undertaken in the colliery's fitting shops. The pair of rails in the foreground of the view to the right allowed colliery tube access to the shops for moving materials and equipment about or, for that matter, for the repair of the much abused tubs themselves. *E. Runicles, courtesy F. Webb*

Part of the main generating plant being brought into the fitting shops for attention. *Courtesy I. J. Brown*

Another view inside the fitting shop showing the tinsmiths' area divided off. *E. Runicles, courtesy F. Webb*

small sum was stopped from their pay each week to contribute to the new facilities.

By 1929 the underground water problem had been taken in hand, after a peak of 1,104 million gallons in 1928, and the coal seams were being pumped dry considerably ahead of the coal face. This meant that the coal being won was dry, which enabled the installation of a pneumatic dry cleaning plant to separate the coal from the shale and dust. This plant was installed around 1930/31.

In 1933 new headframes were built over the shafts, the reinforced concrete replacements being erected around the old timber ones. It is said that in the changeover from the old to the new headframes not a single production shift was lost. The fitting of the new wheels and the changeover

Two views of the ventilation fan house alongside the No. 2 pit. (The view on page 261 shows the fan in place before the completion of the building.) Its purpose was to force fresh air through the underground workings, the No. 2 headframe over the 'upcast' shaft being totally enclosed so that the foul air could be drawn up by the fan. The No. 1 shaft was the 'downcast' where fresh air was drawn down. By closing doors at the pit bottom and at the ends of certain roadways, the air could be forced around the workings via different routes each day. Another ventilating fan for Cannop was situated over the old Wimberry Colliery shaft further up Wimberry Slade.

E. Runicles, courtesy F. Webb

In 1933 the original timber headframes were replaced by concrete ones built by a German firm who did all the shuttering and reinforcing, the concrete being mixed by colliery labourers. As illustrated, the new headframes were built around the old ones, this photograph probably being taken on the Sunday that the new headframes came into use, as a winding wheel can be seen being lifted into place. *E. Runicles, courtesy F. Webb*

of the winding ropes were carried out on a Sunday, which was the maintenance and dirt winding day.

In December 1934 and November 1935 coal was being wound at over 510 tons a shift and, while 3-shift winding was being worked from 1936-1940, production in 1937 totalled 402,784 tons and in 1940 349,353 tons. The 1937 total was the highest ever achieved.

Cannop's problem with water appears to have reversed, as in January 1935 it seems that there was not enough water to feed the boilers! The company wrote to the Crown requesting permission to dam the Cannop Brook to a depth of 4 feet to provide a reservoir. This was granted and a concrete-lined pond was built. The water pumped from the colliery now came into this pond after passing through either the boilers or the baths.

Before reaching the pond, the water passed through the 'sprays'. These were fountains of water which allowed all the sediment and other matter in the water to settle out before the still warm water was piped under the road and down a concrete spillway the length of the pond to enter at its upper end. The slightly warm nature of the water made the pond an attractive bathing place to locals and, in consequence, it became known as the 'Cannop Lido'!

In 1938 the Cannop Coal Co. had a minor brush with the Joint Committee when a 300 yard stretch of railway subsided between Serridge Junction and Miery Stock. The subsidence was blamed on the colliery workings, the area in

Ernest Runicles, pictured between the winding wheels at the top of the No. 1 pit headframe, took the majority of the photographs of Cannop included in this section. The main winding rope passing over the right-hand wheel was built up of 189 strands of steel round a hemp core. *E. Runicles, courtesy F. Webb*

question having been worked under between 1926 and 1934 at a depth of 450 yards.

The Woodbine siding agreement had been terminated on 31st July 1940 as, with the fall in output, it was no longer required, although the Joint Committee retained it for the storage of empties in order that extra wagons could be supplied at short notice. Timber traffic had also increased at the time and large quantities of pit props were loaded by

Another view of the ventilation fan house seen on the previous page, but slightly earlier with the building under construction. The nature of the fan itself can clearly be seen. *E. Runicles, courtesy F. Webb*

The empty wagon roads in the final years.

Keith Allford

the Ministry of Supply at Speech House Road until September 1942, when an alternative loading bank was built by the Military authorities at Mierystock. This seems to have been conveniently timed as 'very heavy incoming traffic' was expected shortly afterwards at Speech House Road.

The final major change at Cannop concerned the management, with the formation of the National Coal Board in 1947. Cannop, like the other major collieries in the Forest, was nationalised and control passed from the hands of the Maclean family to the Government. For the men it meant little difference except that one ex-Cannop collier recalls that his first pay packet from the NCB was 12/6d short — the first time that this had happened!

The colliery continued under the management of the NCB until final closure in September 1960, with the last traffic being worked out of the sidings on 21st November. It has been said that a vast acreage of coal remained untouched, but it was undoubtedly the high cost of pumping water from the colliery which forced its closure.

This study was taken towards the end of the colliery's life, with the land sales wharf on the right.

Forest of Dean Newspapers Ltd.

Looking west over the road underbridge with the Wimberry branch on the left. The loaded wagon weighbridge can be seen just over the bridge. This was built at the colliery's cost, being sanctioned by the Joint Committee in September 1912. The weighing machine itself was replaced in 1938 by one of 50 tons capacity at a cost of £268. In July 1914 the attention of the Joint Committee was drawn to the fact that the colliery was experiencing difficulties at times in working wagons by gravity from the screens to the loaded sidings due to the sharpness of the curve on the weighbridge siding. The Committee's engineer pointed out that 'the flattening of the curve would require the removal of the weighbridge and weighbridge house at a cost of £150'. The colliery company objected to bearing this cost, saying that it was the fault of the railway engineer when laying the sidings in the first place, but the Joint Committee held their ground, pointing out that the colliery's engineer had approved the work and that they should not have to bear the costs of subsequent improvements to the colliery's internal workings. The arguments continued until July 1915 when the colliery company were informed that there had been no default on behalf of the Joint Committee, a view borne out by the general managers of the Great Western and the Midland Railway, the former having been approached direct by the colliery. It is, however, unknown if any alterations were carried out. Certainly in later years several wagons ran away from the screens, at least one reaching the catch points in the sidings where it was thrown off, spreading its load of 3″ nut coal about. The incident happened right at the end of a shift so that those responsible for setting the wagon on its way avoided having to shovel its contents up! Generally some 3-4 loaded wagons were coupled together and allowed to gravitate to the sidings with men running alongside to pin down the brakes.

R. Dagley-Morris

An unidentified pannier tank shunting loaded wagons while its fireman pulls more coal forward from a depleted bunker, presumably towards the end of his turn of duty, on 26th March 1948. Some of the colliery buildings can be seen through the trees in the background.

L. E. Copeland

Looking southwards back towards Speech House Road with the Cannop Colliery sidings on the right and the Wimberry branch on the extreme right beyond them. The difference in the levels of the sidings and the main line is noticeable with the main line climbing towards the camera at 1 in 50 before steeping to 1 in 40 on the bank to Drybrook Road. The junction for the branch to Speech House Hill Colliery was sited just behind the camera.

L. E. Copeland

Speech House Hill Colliery photographed on 12th May 1887 when it was known as Great Western Colliery. The horse-drawn colliery tramway in the foreground is believed to have extended to near Speech House Road station. *Collection A. K. Pope*

SPEECH HOUSE HILL COLLIERY

The early years of Royal Forester gale, which was to become Speech House Hill Colliery, are somewhat obscure. In April 1832 a Richard James of Whitecroft applied to the Crown for the gale but it was not granted to him. Undeterred he erected buildings and commenced work 'at considerable cost' and his right to work the gale was confirmed by the Awards of 1841.

In January 1847 Cornelius and Francis Brain, as lessees of the adjoining Rose-in-Hand gale, were applying for an extension of time for beginning work and it was stated that they had bought Royal Forester in order to drive a level through it to drain Rose-in-Hand. In July 1856 an application was made to the Crown by the registered owners of Rose-in-Hand, Ephraim Brain and John Holingsworth, to make a tramroad connection to the Severn & Wye by means of an incline parallel to the Coleford-Cinderford road. It would appear, however, that this was not constructed until 1869, by which time Royal Forester was owned by the Speech House Hill Colliery Co. (Rose-in-Hand was to become part of Trafalgar Colliery, remaining in the ownership of the Brain family.)

In Severn & Wye minutes it was reported that Messrs. Lückes & Nash, of the Whitecroft Patent Fuel works (see Volume 1, page 120), were representing the Speech House

Hill Colliery Co. and were asking for a quotation on coal rates from the colliery to Parkend and Whitecroft.

In 1873 the Great Western (Forest of Dean) Coal Consumers Co. Ltd. was set up with the objective of taking over the Royal Forester and Cannop Bridge Level gales. The directors of the new concern were Edwin Crawshay, H. R. Lückes, F. Nash, G. W. Owen, A. J. Skinner and W. Wylie. The prospectus issued by the company invited applications for 6,000 shares of £20 each. It also stated that the two collieries, together with all plant, machinery, engines, buildings, stock etc., could be had for £80,000. The extent of the gales was some 400 acres, which it was estimated contained over six million tons of coal. The two shafts had been sunk in the crop of the coal which had proved the quality and value of the seams and it was proposed to deepen the shafts to the Churchway High Delf seam.

In March 1874 Edwin Crawshay, as chairman of the company, approached the Severn & Wye about laying a branch to the pit. Crawshay offered the prospect of a hundred thousand tons of coal traffic per year, but laid heavy emphasis on the expense to be incurred by the colliery in laying sidings, and intimated that they were considering sinking two pits near the Forest of Dean Central line at Foxes Bridge to avoid a steep underground pitching between the coal face and the existing pit bottom. Concerned at the possible loss of such lucrative traffic to the Great Western, the S & W agreed to loan rails, sleepers,

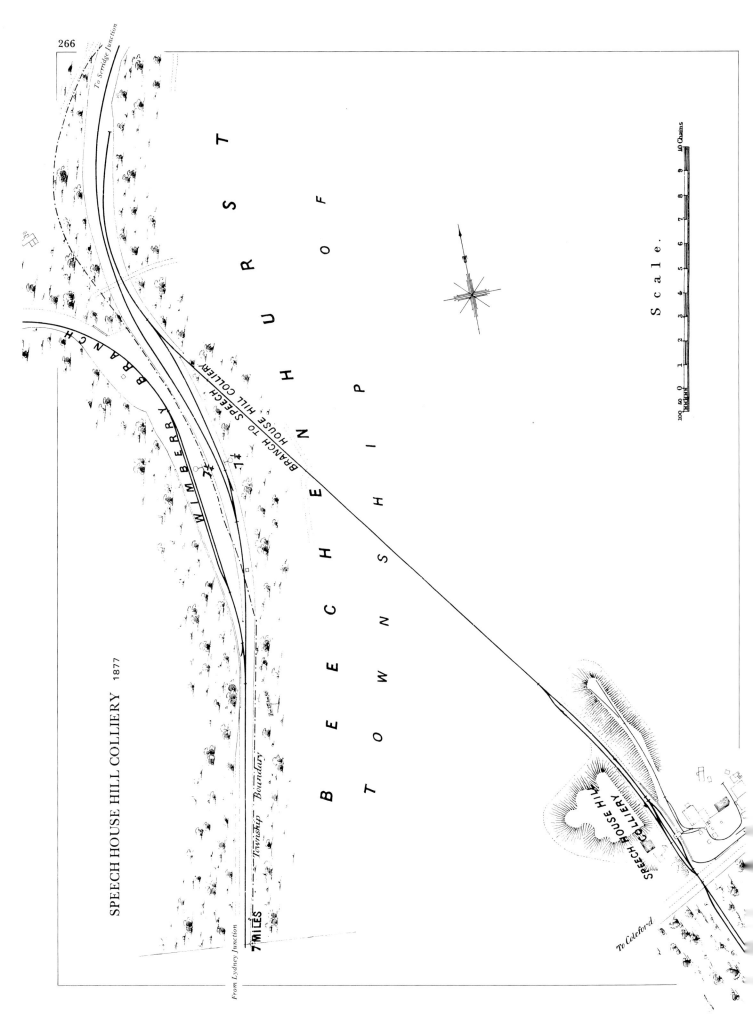

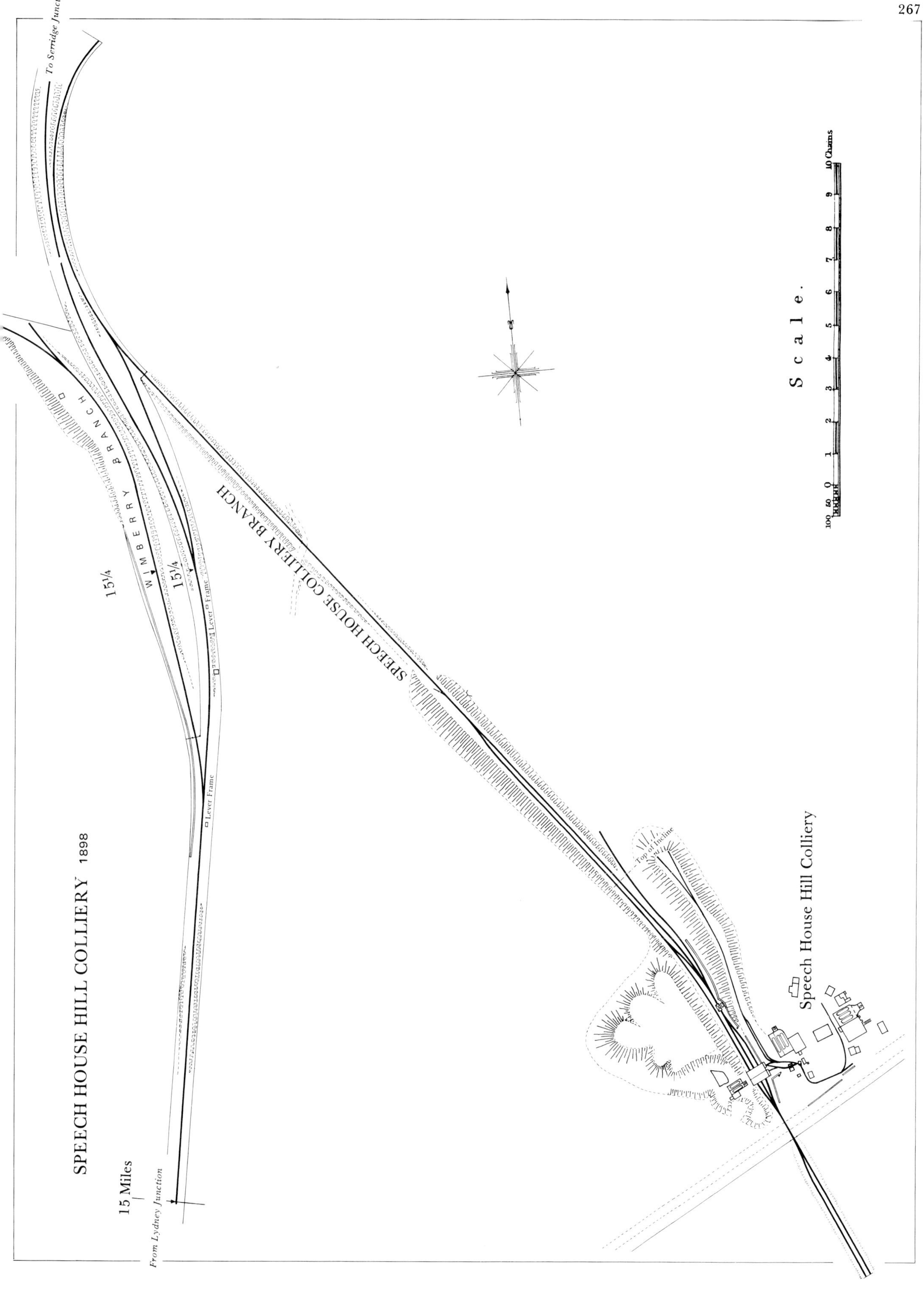

SPEECH HOUSE HILL COLLIERY 1898

15 Miles

15¼

15¼

From Lydney Junction

To Serridge Junction

WIMBERRY BRANCH

SPEECH HOUSE COLLIERY BRANCH

Lever Frame

Lever Frame

Top of Incline

Speech House Hill Colliery

S c a l e .

100 50 0   1   2   3   4   5   6   7   8   9   10 Chains

A general view of the pit-head buildings believed to have been taken around 1896. The photograph is interesting in that it is the only known view of the colliery's own locomotive, believed to have been built by Dick & Stevenson of Airdrie.   *Public Records Office*

etc. if the necessary earthworks were done by the colliery company. Following further discussions, it was decided to let the construction of the branch, and by July 1874 J. E. Billups was appointed contractor. Part of the estimated cost of £3,300 was met by the Severn & Wye whose committee, on 5th April 1875, were conveyed to the colliery where they 'had the satisfaction to find the Branch Line leading thereto as well as the Colliery Works in good order. This colliery is now delivering excellent coal upon our line.'

The first few years following the opening of the branch were punctuated by the efforts of Edwin Crawshay to persuade the Severn & Wye to grant rebates on the colliery's traffic in order to build up its business. By August 1876 Crawshay was urging the S & W to agree through rates with the GWR, stating that he could raise 4,000 tons a month at Speech House Hill 'if he had the trade'.

The Great Western Coal Consumers Co. obviously went through a bad patch in 1878 when it was reported that Messrs. Lückes and Nash, who were 'one time members of the Board of the company', were £24,628 15s 0d in debt. This included £16,000 relating to a guarantee held and claimed by the Gloucestershire Banking Co. from the directors of the company. However, the storm was weathered and by 1881 traffic from the colliery had greatly increased and it was estimated that 12,000 tons a month could soon be produced. This increase in traffic rendered the siding accommodation inadequate and Edwin Crawshay applied to the Severn & Wye for assistance in providing extra track.

The railway responded by offering to lend rails and sleepers for 200 yards of track as long as the colliery company did all the necessary work. However, when Crawshay did not find this acceptable G. W. Keeling replied that the alternative would be to increase the siding accommodation upon railway owned ground at the junction of the colliery branch.

In July 1884 it was recorded in Severn & Wye minutes that the Speech House Hill Colliery had been purchased by the Great Western Collieries Company. In February 1885 the managing director and principal shareholder in this concern, R. Toomer, founder of Messrs. R. Toomer & Co. of Reading, was in difficulty at Speech House Hill owing to an accumulation of small coal. The Severn & Wye were asked if they could assist by giving a special rate on 2,000 tons to Highbridge, Somerset, and, as a result, the colliery was given a rebate of 6d per ton on the normal rate. In April 1887 the Severn & Wye were once again being approached for assistance in providing extra siding accommodation at the colliery.

By 1888 it would seem that the colliery was in some difficulty. The company was in dispute with the adjoining Trafalgar Colliery over an influx of water into Speech House Hill which, it was alleged, came from Trafalgar. The Speech House management thought it due to the cessation of pumping at 'Old Bobs' by the Trafalgar company and, in order to protect the Speech House Hill Colliery from any future water problems from this direction, the proprietors bought the New Mill Engine gale from Trafalgar.

The branch from the colliery descended to the main line on a 1 in 30 gradient and to protect the main line a runaway siding, which rose towards Serridge Junction, was provided. In April 1889 it was decided to lengthen this siding by 40 feet 'for safety' and this necessitated obtaining some extra land from the Crown.

Following the bankruptcy and death of Toomer, the colliery company went into liquidation in April 1892. However, a Severn & Wye minute of May 1892 asks whether or not the liquidation was compulsory 'or only by way of getting rid of some of their shareholders'. In January the Severn & Wye secretary reported as to the progress of the liquidation and produced an application for credit from the Speech House Collieries Company Limited, which was agreed to.

The Great Western Collieries Co. Ltd. had been bought by a Moses Hayes who in turn sold it to the Speech House Collieries Co. Ltd., taking 50 shares in the new concern. The prospectus of the Speech House Collieries Co. Ltd. listed the concern as comprising the Royal Forester, New Mill Engine, Cannop Bridge Level and Prince Albert gales. Work was being done in the Upper series of coals with the Smith Coal, Lowrey, Starkey, Rockey, Churchway, No Coal and Brazilly seams, covering 2,189 acres and containing an estimated 5,205,300 tons of unworked coal.

The Lower series coals, as yet unworked from Speech House Hill, comprised the Yorkley, Whittington, Coleford High Delf and Trenchard seams, with estimated reserves of 6,750,000 tons.

The chairman of the company was Joseph Seekings and the directors included Edgar Jarrett and John Gunter. The price agreed for the sale of the colliery was around £8,500 and the transaction was completed by March 1894.

Upon payment of £207 10s 0d., the new company also acquired 40 wagons, worth £1,200, with future 'deferred payment' instalments amounting to £578 5s 0d. It would also seem that as well as those mentioned, the company also hired wagons. Certainly in 1891 the Great Western Collieries Co. had hired 92 trucks.

The Severn & Wye working appendix of July 1894 shows how the colliery was serviced at that time. Empties were brought to the colliery by the 7.00 a.m. from Lydney, and loaded wagons were picked up by the 10.30 a.m. Drybrook Road to Lydney. Empties were again delivered by the 1.00 p.m. from Coleford Junction to Wimberry and loaded wagons were removed by the 5.30 p.m. ex-Serridge Junction. This suggests that the traffic may have been put into and taken out of the runaway siding, leaving the colliery's own locomotive to work the wagons up and down to the pit head.

The new owners of the colliery were, however, soon in difficulties. In December 1895, following a reduction in wages, 517 men and boys were locked out and by August 1896 the company was in liquidation. The reasons given for this were that the company had failed to carry out their scheme for deepening the pits and working the lower measures and they also neglected to obtain a large additional area. The owners stated that they would continue pumping for three months only and they notified Messrs. Crawshay, who worked the neighbouring Lightmoor Colliery, of this intention.

The sale of the undertaking was scheduled to take place on 21st August 1896, but no buyer could be found. On the 29th it was bought by Mr. W. Alfred Holbrow of Stroud, a former director, and in September he stated: 'I feel that I am taking upon myself very considerable trouble and responsibility but it seemed a great pity that after such a loss on the part of all of us the whole thing should stop when possibly a little more time and one more effort might float it once more.' In an attempt to re-start work, he tried to form a syndicate together with another former director, John Gunter. At this time the colliery consisted of the Royal Forester, Cannop Level and New Mill Engine gales in the upper measures and Prince Albert, New Alexandra, Serridge and United Deep in the lower measures.

In October 1896 Holbrow managed to find a new buyer for the colliery and sold out to a Mr. Whittaker of Keighley, Yorkshire. In November the *Dean Forest Mercury* reported that the underground workings were being repaired and cleaned up, but it was not until July 1898 that the *Dean Forest Guardian* reported that the Speech House Colliery 'after being idle for so long' was about to be re-started. A company under the title of 'The Speech House Main Collieries Company Ltd' had been set up with its registered offices in Temple Buildings, Keighley. It was also reported that J. J. Joynes, the manager of Wimberry Colliery, was to have oversight of the new undertaking.

In 1899 the Speech House Main Collieries Co. purchased another of the deep gales, Union and Cannop, intending

A pair of Speech House Hill wagons. The upper was built by the Gloucester Railway Carriage & Wagon Co. for the Speech House Collieries Co. Ltd., whilst the lower wagon was built for their successors, the Speech House Main Collieries Co. Ltd., by Charles Roberts of Wakefield, Yorkshire. The ornate livery of the latter wagon must be viewed with caution, as it was by no means unknown for wagon manufacturers to turn out a single highly decorated wagon to impress their customers. Liveries carried in traffic were generally a somewhat simplified, and therefore less expensive, version such as that carried on the GRC & W Co. wagon.

GRC & W Co. & HMRS

Looking down the hill showing the rear of the winding engine house. This view was taken after the cessation of coal production at Speech House, the shaft and winding gear being kept as an emergency exit from Lightmoor Colliery.   *Collection N. Parkhouse*

initially to work it from the existing shafts by means of cross measures and later by sinking a new shaft. The cross measure, however, hit a considerable amount of water and work in the area was stopped. Water was to bring more problems to the company when, in August 1901, Henry Crawshay & Co. was once again worried about the build-up of water, which had been deliberately allowed to occur, against the barrier with Lightmoor. Once again the owners of Speech House Hill were in difficulties, and in March 1903 the *Dean Forest Guardian* carried the news that Speech House Hill Colliery had been bought by the Crawshays. The Speech House Main Collieries Co. had gone into liquidation and the purchase was completed on 2nd March. On the 20th the *Dean Forest Mercury* reported that a good deal of interest had been evoked by the purchase, and this was deepened by the fact that the colliery, with its chequered career, was a concern in which an enormous sum of money had been lost. The report continued to say that some 90 men were employed by Crawshay's to get things a little straight as both above and below ground the colliery was in a most unsatisfactory condition.

In April 1903 Crawshay's applied to the Crown to work the barrier between Lightmoor and Speech House Hill. Permission was granted and work commenced, but in July 1904 a large feeder of water was struck. As has already been seen, it was around this time that Crawshay's sold two of the lower measure gales to the syndicate forming the Cannop Colliery Co. These gales were the Prince Albert and the Union and Cannop.

With the opening up of the barrier from Lightmoor, there was no need to maintain the surface works at Speech House Hill. The colliery was disused by 1906 and the points at the junction of the branch were spiked. The connection was not removed until 1909, which led to Messrs. Henry Crawshay & Co. protesting in July 1910 that the value of the colliery premises had been depreciated and that, in the event of a breakdown at Lightmoor Colliery, it might have been necessary to pass traffic over the junction once more.

The Joint Committee, having examined the circumstances, found no reason to restore the connection but agreed to make proper arrangements for working the branch once more should traffic be offered. The track on the branch up the incline and in the colliery yard area remained *in situ* until July 1914 when it was reported that Crawshay's had taken up the whole of their sidings and fenced off their property from that of the Joint Committee, the latter consequently recovering the remaining trackwork upon their own land.

The rails left in place where the sidings crossed the Coleford-Cinderford road were lifted in 1916. Of the surface buildings, some were removed in 1908 and the re-usable materials were taken to Lightmoor. The main shaft and headframe were maintained as an emergency exit for Lightmoor until Crawshay's surrendered Royal Forester gale in April 1937.

Two views looking towards Serridge Junction and showing remains of the Speech House Colliery branch. The upper photograph shows the wide formation where the colliery incline once came down whilst the lower view, taken slightly further north, shows the site of the colliery runaway siding on the right.

Keith Allford

A southbound train descending Serridge bank.   *Keith Allford*

Looking towards Serridge with the commencement of the 1 in 40 gradient round the curve. This stretch of line was on embankment most of the way to Serridge Junction. The signal is the up distant for Speech House Road.   *Roy Denison*

16XX class pannier tank No. 1627 working hard up the 1 in 40 to Serridge on 5th May 1960.

A. K. Pope

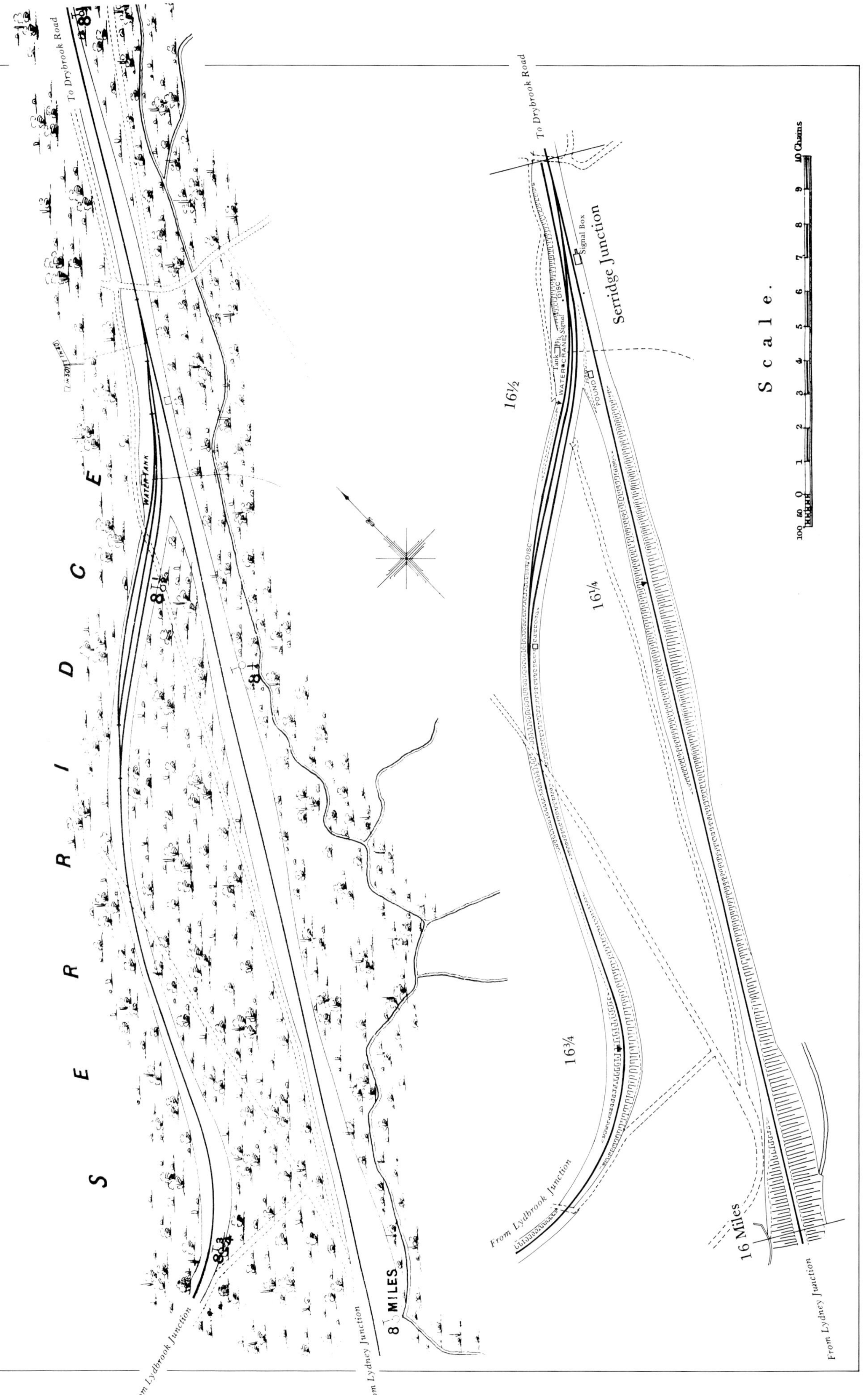

SERRIDGE JUNCTION 1877 and 1898 track plans

S E R R I D G E

To Drybrook Road

From Lydbrook Junction

Water Tank

8.9

8.1
80
8.1

8.4

From Lydney Junction

8 MILES

To Drybrook Road

Serridge Junction

Signal Box

WATER CRANE

Tank

DISC

Signal

DISC

POUND

16½

16¼

16¾

From Lydbrook Junction

16 Miles

From Lydney Junction

S c a l e .

100 60 0   1   2   3   4   5   6   7   8   9   10 Chains

Serridge Junction signal box in 1930.

Collection Keith Allford

SERRIDGE JUNCTION

This remote railway outpost was set amidst some of the most beautiful forest landscape. Indeed, any walker stumbling across the attractive signal box and water tower nestling in the ferns while savouring the delights of his surroundings might be forgiven for mistaking this junction between the Lydbrook branch and the Severn & Wye main line for an innocent and even idyllic railway setting. However, as far as operation was concerned, this was far from the case.

The junction at Serridge came into being when the Lydbrook branch was opened for traffic in August 1874, the line to Drybrook Road having opened in June 1872 as part of the Mineral Loop. When passenger services were introduced in 1875 Lydbrook trains were not allowed to reverse at Serridge and so had to proceed to Drybrook Road for the engine to run round its train and reverse direction for the junction. Later with the extension of passenger services to Cinderford, the return journey past the junction was considerably longer! This operating procedure led to A. O. Cooke writing in 1913 to say:

> Certainly the railway journey is leisurely in the extreme. From Speech House Road station we pass through Drybrook Road and reach Cinderford. Thence, after several bustling manoeuvres on the part of the little engine, we travel back to Drybrook Road and past Trafalgar Colliery. At Serridge Junction the train, hitherto running south-west now leaves the Speech House line and bends sharply round by Speculation Colliery, heading due north towards Upper Lydbrook.

A platform was provided at Serridge in 1878 for the use of the keeper at Serridge Lodge. Undoubtedly because of the unrelenting climb to Drybrook Road only 'down' trains called after the guard had been notified, but it seems it was little used and last appeared in 'Bradshaw' in October 1879. The platform was situated on the 'up' side close to where a forest ride crossed the line.

It was goods and mineral traffic which brought activity to Serridge Junction. Coal from Mierystock and other collieries and works on the Lydbrook branch, and traffic exchanged with the GWR at Lydbrook Junction, had to be remarshalled here for the reversal to Lydney. Clearly the situation was far from satisfactory, not least from the aspect of safety, as quite apart from the gradient at the commencement of the Lydbrook branch, the main line itself was on a 1 in 40 gradient at this point. However, it was not until October 1910 that increasing traffic prompted officers of the Joint Committee to meet on site to consider the question of providing additional accommodation to alleviate the problem. The engineer was requested to prepare plans of the necessary accommodation to avoid the practice of forming trains on the main line. At a subsequent meeting the following April it was explained that the difficulties in dealing with traffic at Serridge had been considerably increased by the output from the new Mierystock pits, which then reached some 5,000 tons a month, and that additional accommodation was urgently required. The engineer's plan was produced for the work, which was estimated at £4,322 including signalling, and it was agreed to recommend the expenditure. However, it was not until

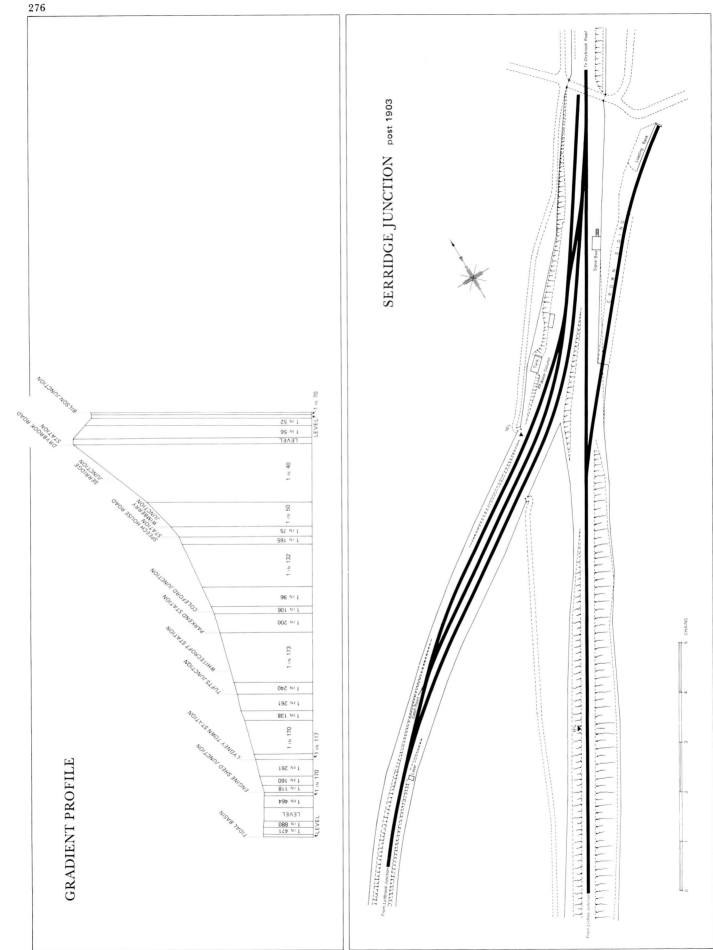

GRADIENT PROFILE

SERRIDGE JUNCTION post 1903

A guard's view over a train of empties approaching Serridge on 26th March 1948.

L. E. Copeland

the following January that the secretary could report that the general managers had agreed the scheme should be proceeded with and this time at an estimated £4,402 including signalling. This provided for:

'1. The construction of a siding capable of holding 40 wagons, enabling the marshalling of trains on a section of the main line with a heavy gradient to be discontinued.
2. The utilisation of the excavated soil in the formation of a bank upon which a new straight running road in the direction of Lydbrook can be laid, when the existing line can be converted into a siding for 50 wagons.
3. The renting from the Crown of additional land, to the extent of 3 acres, 1 rood, 33 poles, at the usual rate of £2 an acre.'

The work was not proceeded with immediately and in October 1913 the traffic manager reported that owing to a want of funds, the Lydney and Crump Meadow Collieries Co. Ltd. had not been able to develop their Mierystock Colliery as anticipated and as the Pluds pit, which had formerly output 50 wagons per day, had been closed, he recommended that the scheme be 'deferred for the present'. He did, however, still consider it advisable to provide a shunting neck for marshalling trains.

The matter was again deferred until a new plan and estimate could be prepared, but in the event it was agreed, on 14th July 1914, that 'the circumstances do not justify the large expenditure involved in providing the shunting neck separately from the other work', and there the matter rested.

It therefore fell to the train crews to continue to operate the junction safely, dependent on their own skills to cope with the problems. It seems the most tricky operation was handling loaded coal trains from Mierystock to Lydney. On arrival at Serridge the train would stop on the running line and, when the wagons were secured, the locomotive would run round to the rear of the train to collect the brake van. It would then run round the brake van using the third loop siding and put it onto the opposite end of the train. The locomotive would then run round again to couple to the opposite end of the train which was thus reformed for the reverse direction to Lydney. The difficult part of the operation was to propel the train onto the main line sufficiently clear of the junction points and fouling bar to enable the signalman to change them before the momentum of the ascending loaded wagons was lost and they rolled back down the gradient, forcing the loco back down the bank, hopefully on its way to Lydney.

This was a difficult task for all concerned and co-ordination was vital. The manoeuvre began by hauling the train back up the Lydbrook branch to Speculation Curve in order to get a run at the opposing gradient on the main line. The driver then held the regulator wide open and stormed back down the branch, propelling the wagons for all he was worth past the sidings and onto the 1 in 40 bank on the main line. This must have been quite a spectacle. As their van passed the signal box the two guards jumped off ready to pin down the wagon brakes to help hold the train on the gradient, and, the very instant the loco was clear of the points, the vigilant signalman set the road for Lydney. However, things did not always go according to plan and

278

Looking south over the junction from the up home bracket signal on 24th August 1946 with the 'up' token catching apparatus just visible at the bottom of this view. The small corrugated iron lamp hut at the foot of the steps was provided in 1907. The reported inadequacy of lighting arrangements at certain junctions and sidings prompted representatives of the parent companies to visit various sites during the summer of 1914. Serridge was subsequently included in their general recommendation but presumably the intervention of the Great War prevented the four oil lamps authorised from being installed until January 1917, the completed work costing £42 5s. 2d. Unfortunately their location is not apparent as they would appear to have been removed by the time these pictures were taken.

L. E. Copeland

Looking north from the gallery of the down home signal featured in the view on page 277 and showing the Crown siding heading off through the undergrowth on the other side of the gate towards the loading bank. One Lydney driver remembers pit props being loaded at the siding as often as once a week. However, with the fluctuation of this traffic the siding was sometimes unused for some weeks or even months.
L. E. Copeland

often, particularly in poor weather, the whole procedure had to be started all over again, and possibly several times. Former staff remember one driver who could never get it right!

The reverse operation with, for instance, empties for Mierystock, was much easier, a train from Lydney continuing up the bank until it was clear of the junction and reversing into the sidings. The locomotive then had to collect the brake van and run round it, thus using all three lines again to re-form the train for the opposite direction. Sometimes, if there were too many empties for the climb to Mierystock, some were left in the siding and a second trip was made.

CROWN SIDING

By an agreement dated 2nd August 1872 between the Office of Woods and the Severn & Wye, the latter were placed under an obligation to 'provide loading places for timber and bark and other materials at Mierystock and Whitegates'. However, in December 1901 it was agreed that the proposed siding at Whitegates should instead be made at Serridge Junction where it could be under the immediate control of the signalman in Serridge Junction signal box.

The first proposal to install the siding was in January 1903 and by 25th May the rails were in place to the satisfaction of the railway but not, unfortunately, to that of the Crown. They stated that, whilst the rails had been put in at the place agreed upon, the siding was left in such a way that

Signalman Hough inside Serridge box c.1930. A later signalman here would not remain in his box whilst a train was being propelled off the Lydbrook line. He was worried that should the guard's van jump the rails then the entire train would come through the box!
Collection Keith Allford

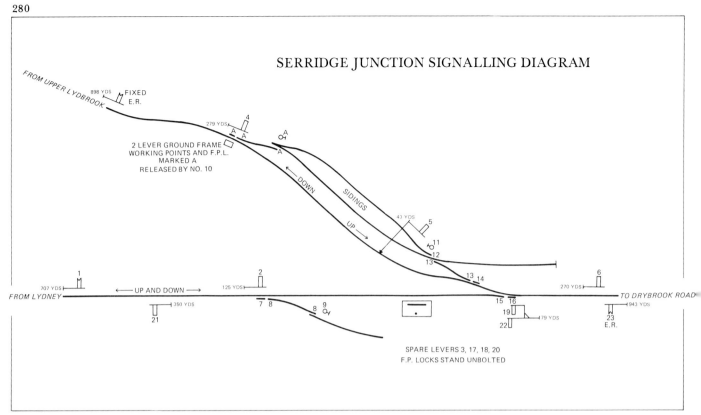

SERRIDGE JUNCTION SIGNALLING DIAGRAM

FROM UPPER LYDBROOK

898 YDS — FIXED E.R.

279 YDS

4

A A

2 LEVER GROUND FRAME
WORKING POINTS AND F.P.L.
MARKED A
RELEASED BY NO. 10

A
A

DOWN

SIDINGS

UP →

43 YDS

5

11

12

13

13 14

1

2

6

FROM LYDNEY — ← UP AND DOWN → 125 YDS

707 YDS

270 YDS

TO DRYBROOK ROAD

350 YDS

21

7 8

8 9

15 16

19

22

79 YDS

23
E.R.

943 YDS

SPARE LEVERS 3, 17, 18, 20
F.P. LOCKS STAND UNBOLTED

A 1930s view of the signal cabin, the superstructure of which is believed to have been salvaged from Lydney Town in 1897. It seems to have been staffed throughout the day's timetable by one man until February 1897 when an extra signal porter was appointed to bring staff hours to within 12 per day.

L. E. Copeland

The signalman's view over the proceedings.

Collection Keith Allford

it was useless as a loading point for the Crown. No space was left on either side onto which a wagon could be hauled and no loading bank had been constructed 'for the convenient loading into railway trucks of timber, bark, etc.' It was also stated that some bark had already been sold on the understanding that it could be loaded at Serridge and that unless this could be done it would involve the Crown in a considerable financial loss. The Crown therefore wrote to the Joint Committee requesting that a 'proper loading bank be constructed forthwith'.

The Joint Committee, however, contended that by laying the siding they had fulfilled their part of the agreement. The Crown took the stand that the siding was not to the satisfaction of their deputy surveyor and that the Joint Committee should be liable to provide the loading bank. It was decided that, in order to avoid the delay involved in discussions on the matter, the loading bank should be constructed immediately without prejudice to the question of which party would eventually bear the cost.

This appears to have been acceptable to the Joint Committee as on 27th May their engineer was instructed to commence work on the loading bank. The Crown's deputy surveyor reported on 13th July that it 'was to some extent made' but that all the bark waiting to be loaded had been hauled away before the bank was in a usable state. He pointed out that the time involved in constructing it was due to the fact that there was only one man and one labourer employed upon it rather than a proper gang.

The loading bank was reported as complete on 6th August 1903, although in the opinion of a local officer of the Office of Woods it was not of sufficient length! The siding, inspected by the Board of Trade and passed fit for use on 14th August, connected into the 1 in 40 gradient of the main line and thus required special working regulations. The following is an extract from the 1911 Working Appendix:-

> The siding has been provided for the accommodation of Customers of the Crown for loading Timber and Bark and other produce from Crown lands. As the point of connection with the Main Line is on a falling gradient of 1 in 40 in the direction of Speech House Road Station, the following instructions must be strictly observed:-
>
> 1. All Wagons put into or taken out of the Siding must be worked from and to Serridge Junction Sidings on the Lydbrook Branch, and no passing train must be allowed to do any work at the Siding.
> 2. No Vehicle must be placed into or taken out of the Siding unless the Engine is on the lower or Speech House Road end of such Vehicle, and under no circumstances must any Vehicle be left on the Main Line during the time the Engine is engaged in the Siding, and before any Wagons are taken from the Serridge Sidings on the Lydbrook Branch to the Crown Siding, the Guard in charge of the operation must first make room by clearing out any Wagons required, taking care, in conjunction with the Driver, to see that there are not more Vehicles attached to the Engine than can conveniently be propelled up the gradient into the Siding, after passing over the points, or brought to a stand by the brake on the Engine and those on the Trucks, should occasion arise.

No. 2043 easing a loaded coal train slowly down the bank from Speculation curve on 26th March 1948. The tablet (later token) catching apparatus in the foreground was authorised in October 1900. The water tank replaced an old wooden one which probably dated from the first provision of a water supply in 1874 and which, in October 1895, was described as 'being much out of repair'. As with Coleford and Lydbrook Junction, the replacement iron one featured here was estimated at £60 'delivered at Swindon exclusive of fixing'. The cost of 'fixing the new iron tanks on masonry to replace those worn out' was estimated at £130, presumably for the three, but whether this included building the base or whether the masonry already existed to support the old wooden tanks is not clear. The supply was gravity fed and in 1904 £30 was spent in repairing or renewing the supply and repairing a small reservoir. Even so, loco crews recall that the supply was unreliable and the tank was often dry. The starting signal next to the tank was included in the list of works required by the Board of Trade prior to the introduction of passenger services, as was a repeater in the signal box to the up distant signal from Drybrook. *L. E. Copeland*

Another view from the signal box as No. 2043 brings the same loaded train from Mierystock to a stand.   *L. E. Copeland*

Having stopped at the home signal, the train was divided.   *L. E. Copeland*

For the final picture of the brief sequence, the photographer has rejoined the guard's van and the guards are seen pinning down the wagon brakes while the loco propels the short train up the steep bank from the sidings where it had been divided and reformed. The train having cleared the junction, the signalman has just reversed the points and pulled off the signal for Lydney. *L. E. Copeland*

An earlier view taken on the same day and showing a train of empties for Mierystock being propelled onto the Lydbrook branch. The starting signal in the distance was authorised in 1903 at a cost of £27, to afford proper protection as the main line was used as a shunting neck. *L. E. Copeland*

L. E. Copeland

This splendid panorama shows the isolated location of the junction on 6th July 1946.

A coal train off the Lydbrook branch about to set off for Lydney. Certainly in later years the 'up' token catcher at the junction was seldom used by southbound trains from Cinderford, tokens being exchanged by hand while the driver observed the speed limit over the facing points.   *Rev. D. A. Tipper*

This snapshot, probably taken before 1929, shows the back of the 'up' distant signal for Serridge as seen before the removal of the junction bracket applying to movements through the curve on to the Lydbrook branch (lever 20), The 'down' distant for Drybrook Road is also featured in the background. The Forest landscape is subject to continual change as a result of Forestry activities as witnessed by comparing this and the next view.

Courtesy Keith Allford

Between Serridge Junction and Drybrook Road where the S & W ran close by a large spoil heap from Trafalgar Colliery, the line was protected by a retaining wall braced at one point by the brick-lined stone arch illustrated. This was built by the Severn & Wye after lengthy negotiations with Trafalgar's owners who, in 1875, informed the S & W that they wished to extend the tip adjacent to the railway. The colliery company suggested that this could only be done by building a bridge to enable spoil to be run across the line and tipped on Crown land on the far side, and that the S & W would be liable for the cost of this. The S & W were quick to forestall this request by pointing out that sufficient space existed for at least another year's tipping on the colliery side of the line. In December the following year the S & W's Board agreed in principle to provide a bridge, but it was not until August 1878 that approval was finally given to erect the bridge at a cost of approximately £200, in lieu of one which the S & W had been under obligation to provide for the accommodation of the colliery near Drybrook Road station. Nothing is known of this earlier agreement, nor is it by any means certain that the bridge built by the railway was in fact used to convey spoil across the line since, in 1887, a serious slip occurred causing damage to the retaining wall estimated at £200. This was

almost certainly caused by pressure from the original tip, and the S & W were quick to remind the colliery company of the need to take adequate precautions to avoid a recurrence. In reply the colliery's owners evidently accused the S & W both of building the railway against their wishes and of not building the bridge to the agreed length. The S & W refuted both claims but it is not recorded who ultimately paid for the repairs. However, in July 1903 the S & W's engineer considered the existing wall ought to be replaced by a stronger one costing some £740. At first the colliery company agreed to supply the necessary dressed stone, estimated at £147, but by the following January, as they had 'discontinued depositing refuse at the existing pit bank', they withdrew their offer and instead offered £100 towards the expense.

The wall was started in April 1904 and completed by October for only £1 16s 1d in excess of the original estimate, but in December 1904 it was reported that the new wall, built under an arrangement of 30th October 1903, had recently fallen down. Rebuilding was postponed until 'some time in the future' when the colliery company commenced tipping again above it. Subsequent events are not clear. This view of Trafalgar Arch was taken on 26th March 1948. The signal is the Serridge Junction up distant (No. 23).

L. E. Copeland

An early view of the pit-head at Trafalgar, believed to have been taken prior to 1879. The photograph is taken from the bridge over the colliery tramway incline to the screens, as shown on the 1877 track plan. The eminent gentlemen standing in the foreground are probably some of the Brain family, the owners of the colliery. The flimsy headframes are prominent on the left and it can be seen that the two shafts were wound from the same winding house. Two of the Brain's Tramway locomotives feature behind the men, probably *Trafalgar* on the right and *The Brothers* to the left, both 0–4–2 tanks built by Lilleshall. The variety of styles of gas lamps is noteworthy.

Dean Heritage & Museum Trust

TRAFALGAR COLLIERY

The Trafalgar gale was granted in August 1842 to Corneleus Brain of Mitcheldean and was to remain in the possession of the Brain family until 1919. It would appear that work did not commence at Trafalgar until around 1860 although it must be said that details of the early history of the concern are few and far between.

As has already been seen, under the history of Speech House Hill Colliery (page 265), Corneleus and Francis Brain were the lessees of the Rose-in-Hand gale, certainly since 1847, and in 1867 they obtained a Crown licence to work the barrier between Rose-in-Hand and Trafalgar gales. This meant that the two gales effectively became one for the purpose of working the coal which would undoubtedly have been raised via the shafts at Trafalgar. No record of a shaft or level on Rose-in-Hand has been found, coal from here, previous to 1867, having been brought to the surface through Royal Forester gale which later formed part of Speech House Hill Colliery.

It is also possible that at around this time the Brains acquired the New Strip-and-at-it Colliery which lay adjacent to Trafalgar. Strip-and-at-it was a concern which had already been worked for a considerable period. The 1841 Awards of Coal and Iron Mines stated that a John Harris had been working Strip-and-at-it since April 1832 although his application for the gale had been rejected. The gale had, however, been surrendered to the Crown in 1864 and was then acquired by the Brains. Strip-and-at-it had been connected to the Churchway branch of the Severn & Wye tramroad in 1842 and, with the commencement of operations at Trafalgar in 1860, permission was gained for a

connection to the Strip-and-at-it spur, the new line including a short tunnel.

At Trafalgar itself there were two shafts down to the Churchway High Delf seam at a depth of 195 yards. They were between 30 and 40 yards apart and worked by the same winding engine, with coal coming up one and empties being lowered down the other.

Trafalgar appears to have been unique amongst Forest collieries in that it was gas-lit underground, this only being possible due to the coalfield's freedom from gas or fire-damp. A *Dean Forest Guardian* report of a visit by Captain and Mrs. Wemyss to Trafalgar in October 1874 reads:

> . . . that with Mr. T. B. Brain descended the shaft in the ordinary skip. In this subterranean passage the visitors had not calculated upon finding the roadways lighted with gas similar to that employed in the lighting of streets and dwellings and were agreeably surprised to find impenetrable darkness, the workings clearly defined from the jet burners which were dotted about the roadways . . . It may be of interest to add that the gas is forced down the shaft by means of a one horse horizontal engine erected in the gas house at the pit bank.

The gas house is the building shown on the 1898 Severn & Wye plans containing a circular structure.

Another account of the gas illumination at Trafalgar comes from a guide book by John Bellows of Gloucester called *A Week's Holiday in the Forest of Dean* and published around 1880. It also gives some details of the surface workings and other facts about Trafalgar.

> Before going down (underground) we may as well look at the large sandstone quarry on the premises where stones are cut for

Brain's Tramway locomotive *Trafalgar*, an 0—4—2T of 2' 7½" gauge built by Lilleshall Iron Co. in 1869.   *Courtesy B. W. E. Waters*

TRAFALGAR COLLIERY 1898 and 1877 track pla

Engine   Ashes

Trafalgar Colliery

16¾

From Lydney Junction

17 Miles

E A N

E

Trafalgar Colliery

From Lydney Junction

8

U   R   E

TRAFALGAR SIDINGS

9 M.

To Drybrook Road

100 50 0   1   2   3   4   5   6   7   8   9   10 Chains

supporting the galleries below. Let us pass through the tramway tunnel, 150 yards long, cut through the ridge of the hilltop, to a shaft on the other side. This narrow ridge is the outcrop of the measures, and in the tunnel we can examine, rock, clod and duns, and a little thin coal with rock again below it. Having seen this we turn back again, enter the cage, and, closing our eyes to avoid the giddiness, are lowered 600 feet so smoothly, that we are hardly conscious of motion. At the bottom we go into the underground office, and are supplied with a little brass lamp, and a bunch of cotton waste to wipe our hands upon, and then attended by 'the bailey' enter one of the main roadways . . .

. . . Where necessary, the underground workings are lighted with gas, and one of the partners, Mr. William Brain, is now preparing to adopt the electric light (which is already in use on the surface at night) and also to utilize electricity as a motive power at many of the underground inclines, or dipples, in the colliery, where steam is not available; and thus save many horses. There are

more than forty horses living in this pit. They never return to daylight until worn out or disabled. Some of them have been down here a dozen years, and are in excellent health.

Fire damp is wholly unknown in the Forest of Dean, and miners work with naked lights. Choke damp breaks in rarely, and seldom gives any trouble. The pit is remarkably free from water, and being furnished with every known appliance, and most admirably kept, is probably one of the best in the Forest, or out of it. Eleven hundred men and boys are employed here: 600 underground getting coal, and 500 as labourers &c., above ground, and in subsidiary occupations. Good colliers earn, at present, 3s 8d per day; masons 3s 4d; and labourers, 2s 4d. One can hardly imagine anything more severe in the way of labour than that of a miner lying on his side in a four foot passage, cutting away with his pick the hard rock encasing the seam . . .

. . . The output from Trafalgar, at the moment we are writing, which is a dull season is seven hundred tons of coal per day.

The foregoing passage gives a reasonable account of Trafalgar Colliery and is also notable in mentioning the use of electricity at the pit.

Francis William Thomas (Frank) Brain had been associated with the use of electric floodlights on the Severn Bridge in 1879 where they had been used to enable construction work to continue at night to make the best use of the tides. After use on the bridge, the apparatus, consisting of a couple of powerful lamps supplied by a Gramme machine, was re-erected at Trafalgar on the surface to light the colliery yard, and a football match was even played at night! Frank Brain was also connected with the Electric Blasting Apparatus Company who made fuses for simultaneous shot firing underground, and had buildings close to Trafalgar Colliery.

Electricity was also used at Trafalgar when the first underground pumping plant was installed in December 1882. It attained such success that three additional plants were erected in May 1887 and these did the larger part of the pumping.

The installation at Trafalgar was the first recorded use of electric power in mines. The equipment consisted of a Gramme machine on the surface driven by a steam engine and a Siemens dynamo used as a 1½ horse power motor belted to a pump underground. The Gramme machine still exists today, preserved in the National Museum of Wales in Cardiff.

Trafalgar was connected to the Severn & Wye at a point between Serridge Junction and Drybrook Road station. The sidings to the screens stemmed from a loop off the main line on the 'down' side. They were laid soon after the Mineral Loop was constructed, Trafalgar Colliery being one of those which it was intended to serve. Agreement was reached in July 1872 for a siding to be put in, the S & W sharing the cost with the colliery, and by November the following year the S & W's chairman and engineer were able to observe 'the effective working of the new coal screens at Trafalgar Colliery which are well reported of'.

Prior to the construction of the Loop, however, Trafalgar was connected to the Great Western Railway at Bilson by a 2' 7½" gauge tramway, known locally as Brain's Tramway. The single line of edge rails laid on wooden sleepers ran east from the colliery, turning south-east at Laymoor, and terminated 1½ miles away at interchange sidings at Bilson. It would appear that the authorisation for its construction was a Crown licence for 'a road or tramway 15 feet broad' dated May 1862. The date the line was opened for traffic is unknown as, although the first of three locomotives used on the tramway was built in 1869, it is possible that it may have been horse worked before this date.

Traffic continued unhindered on the line, with a locomotive hauling 20-25 trams of coal on each trip, until 1872 when the Severn & Wye built their branch to Bilson. This

To Nailbridge

17¼

To Drybrook Road

The missing portion of this 1877 plan was concealed in the binding of the original plans

Looking west towards the corrugated iron clad screens. When the sidings in the foreground were installed in 1890 they cut through the original incline to the old screens (see page 290), the course of which is discernible on the left by the odd lengths of fencing. A rake of loaded wagons is being lowered one by one over the wagon weighbridge and past the long row of colliery empties. The empty Trafalgar wagon, evidently placed by the accompanying shunting horse, is standing on the short siding for interchange with Brain's Tramway which ran down the graded 'shelf' behind the weighbridge office. Trafalgar House is prominent on the horizon of this early photograph which, with the lightweight track in the foreground with its flat-bottomed rail, interlaced sleepering and simple point levers, provides a rare and valuable glimpse of the old Severn & Wye.

Courtesy Jack Aston

The northern end of Brain's Tramway was for many years a land sales wharf at Nailbridge. Here we see a rake of Trafalgar wagons standing on a siding off the Great Western's Forest of Dean branch for which the Trafalgar Colliery Co. took out a siding agreement in July 1897. Brain's Tramway can be seen to the left of the furthest wagon. *Collection N. Parkhouse*

This interesting 0—4—0 tank, built by Lilleshall, is seen here in almost the same position as *Trafalgar.* Given the name *Free Miner*, it is believed to have been built in 1865. Of interest is the riveted plate boiler and the total absence of any lagging. The valve gear is also noteworthy in that it is worked from eccentrics on the rear axle via the cross-shaft behind the rear wheels and the long rod under the tank. The connecting rod is forked just behind the motion bracket and goes either side of the crosshead. The locomotive is coupled to a standard 'dram'. In this view the colliery offices can again be seen on the right with what is believed to have been a two road engine shed on the left. It is possible that a locomotive using electric drive was used at Trafalgar in 1886 as a report in the *Electrical Engineer* of February 1889 states that the power for the locomotive was gained from storage batteries It is, however, unknown whether it was used above or below ground but Brain's Tramway would have been its likely use, especially for shunting in the colliery yard. *Courtesy Jack Aston*

TRAFALGAR COLLIERY

A panorama of the colliery taken between 1907 and 1910. Part of the quarry mentioned in the text can just be seen behind the tall chimney on the left. The building to the right of this housed the electric generating plant whilst the structure with the curved roof, in front of the winding house, accommodated several boilers. A large number of standard gauge wagons can just be discerned in the distance to the right of the headframes.

Collection A. K. Pope

Another view contemporary with that on page 288, showing Trafalgar House, the residence of the Brain family, and part of Brain's Tramway in the foreground.

Dean Heritage Museum Trust

crossed the tramway on the level near Laymoor and it was this crossing which caused problems when the Severn & Wye extended beyond Drybrook Road. When passenger trains began running over it in August 1878, the increased traffic prompted the Brains to complain to the Severn & Wye in November of 'the hindrance and danger to their traffic on the trolley road at its crossing of the Bilson branch'.

Despite this small antagonism, the tramway settled down to a period of peaceful co-existence with the Severn & Wye until, in 1885, the latter decided that far too much of Trafalgar's output was reaching the Great Western over the tramway. An approach was made to the colliery company to provide arrangements for loading hand picked nut coal on the Severn & Wye sidings as well as on the Great Western at Bilson. This was rejected at first but by January 1887, after further negotiations, Trafalgar approved a proposal whereby the Severn & Wye altered the sidings and shed whilst the colliery company altered the screens, thus resolving this 'vexed question'.

Finally, in December 1889, an agreement was entered into between the Severn & Wye and the Trafalgar Colliery Company who, it was said, 'are desirous of obtaining railway communication to Bilson Junction in lieu of their existing trolley road.'

It was agreed that on or before 31 March 1890 the colliery company would construct new sidings and the railway company would lay in a new junction at Drybrook Road. Although the new junction was a quarter of a mile closer to Drybrook Road than the old sidings, the mileage charge was to remain the same. The accommodation, on approximately the same level as Drybrook Road station,

was to be constructed so that traffic to and from the Great Western would be placed on a different siding to that which was to pass over the Severn & Wye system. For taking traffic to Bilson Junction for transfer to the Great Western the colliery was to be charged 7d per loaded wagon, although empties were to pass free. The transfer traffic also had to be conveyed 'at reasonable times and in fair quantities so as to fit in with the ordinary workings of the Railway Company trains'.

The new sidings were brought into use on 1st October 1890 and a circular sent out by the Trafalgar management to traders read:

We have now completed extensive alterations and in future all coal will be loaded by means of improved screens erected at the pits mouth.

It will facilitate our arrangements and ensure the most prompt attention possible if customers will please label their trucks via Severn Bridge and Lydney Junction — Severn and Wye Railway.

As to the working of the sidings, the 1894 Severn & Wye rule book stipulated:

1st. The Main Line Train on arriving at Drybrook Road Junction is to place the Empties into the left hand Siding, and, if the road is clear, to push them on as far as desired by the Colliery Company, provided there is no delay.

2nd. Take out to Drybrook Road Junction all wagons, then loaded and weighed, for the Severn & Wye & Severn Bridge Railway; but, if the load is too heavy, the Wagons left behind must be drawn down to the lower end of the Siding, so as to leave the upper portion of the Siding free for the Colliery to weigh and place their Wagons.

3rd. Take out the Wagons loaded for the Great Western Railway

A closer view of the winding house and headframes.

Collection A. K. Pope

The checkweighman's hut which stood in front of the headframes. The number 96 chalked on the coal in the wooden colliery tubs in the foreground denotes the team which filled that particular tub. The two vertical wooden rods suspended from the front of the headframes located in metal shoes fitted to each cage to guide it down the shaft. The main coal raising shaft to the right of the checkweighman's hut was also the upcast shaft and consequently equipped with a kind of bonnet, as illustrated, to prevent too much air going down the shaft. *Collection A. K. Pope*

to Bilson; returning with the Empties to Trafalgar and placing them as before.

4th. Take out to Drybrook Road Junction the remainder of the Wagons then loaded and weighed for the Severn & Wye & Severn Bridge Railway.

Following the abandonment of the stretch of Brain's Tramway from Laymoor to Bilson Junction, two of the locomotives were put up for sale. An advertisement in the *Colliery Guardian*, 2nd January 1891, read: 'For sale, in consequence of abandonment of pit cart railway, two 6-wheeled locomotives, built by Lilleshall Iron Co. Copper fireboxes, brass tubes. Good working order.' The two locomotives concerned appear to have been *Trafalgar* (built 1869) and *The Brothers* (1870); both were 0—4—2 side tanks with 8 x 14 in. outside cylinders and valve gear. The sale, however, did not go through and both locomotives remained at Trafalgar until broken up.

Trafalgar was in fact in use until 1906 working on the northern extension of the tramway, built in 1869, to the Golden Valley Iron Mine at Drybrook. This extension will be dealt with in a future volume. The third locomotive was *Free Miner* which is also believed to have been built by Lilleshall, but as an 0—4—0.

The level crossing over the Severn & Wye at Laymoor was undoubtedly removed soon after 1890, together with the stretch of line to Bilson Yard. However, this isolated the colliery locomotives from their water supply which had been gained from Laymoor Well. To preserve the facility, pipes were laid under the Severn & Wye to a brick water tank on the north side of the railway. It would appear, however, that this tank was out of use by 1897.

Returning to the affairs of the colliery itself, it seems that by 1913 difficulties were being encountered with water. The managements of both Foxes Bridge and Lightmoor Collieries were worried about the threatened abandonment of Trafalgar; it was feared that if pumping ceased, their own collieries might be under threat from the build-up of water within Trafalgar's workings. The colliery was offered for sale to Crawshay's, the owners of Lightmoor and with an interest in Foxes Bridge, but at a figure they would not entertain.

At the beginning of 1919 the main dip roadway at Trafalgar was suddenly, and unexpectedly, flooded and again the Foxes Bridge and Lightmoor managements were worried about the dangers to their concerns. Trafalgar was now offered for sale at £16,000. The Foxes Bridge and Lightmoor managements were prepared to offer £10,000 and, in an attempt to meet the difference, the Crown agreed to provide £4,000 should the sale go through. It was estimated at this time that there was still 2½ million tons of coal to be worked in the pit and its associated gales which would give the Crown an annual return from tonnage rates of £1,000 for 20 years, certainly paying back the £4,000.

On 4th November 1919 the transfer of the Trafalgar Colliery Co. Ltd. by Sir Francis Brain to Henry Crawshay & Co. Ltd. (represented by Edwin William Morgan) and the Foxes Bridge Colliery Co. Ltd. (represented by Arthur John Morgan) was completed.

The new management obviously continued to work coal from Trafalgar as a total of 4,729 tons were shipped via Lydney and Sharpness in 1923. However, in December of that year it was reported that the colliery was in difficulties for an area of coal to work. An application was made to the Crown to work the barrier between Trafalgar and Foxes Bridge but this was refused.

In June 1924 there were press reports of the formation of the New Trafalgar Colliery Co. Ltd. which it was said

A close-up of a cage at Trafalgar about to descend the shaft. As it went down, the gate above came down to enclose the shaft and prevent anyone falling down it. Colliers travelled up and down on what were called 'bonds' at the start and end of their shifts. Those on the first cage, or bond, earned the privilege of taking the first 'bond' back up. Although only four men are shown here, the permitted load of each cage was 'ten men and boys'. The four chains, by which the cage was attached to the winding rope, were known as 'tacklers'.   *Collection A. K. Pope*

The original generating set viewed around 1883 with what is believed to be Sydney Scott standing behind the engine. This engine was still in use in 1925 working a more modern generating set. The original Gramme machine can be seen at the far end of the building connected to the horizontal steam engine by an eleven strand non-slip rope.

Collection A. K. Pope

This photograph, taken in 1883, shows the engine staff at Trafalgar. The figure seventh from the left was Sidney Scott, the chief engineer. The building behind them housed the then new electric generating plant.

Collection A. K. Pope

A Trafalgar Colliery pay check.

Two views of the later generating set seen around 1903.

Collection A. K. Pope

This old postcard view shows the Strip-and-at-it Colliery situated on the other side of the ridge from Trafalgar itself. This view is from the top of the tramway tunnel which connected the two sites. The shaft nearest the camera was used as an emergency exit from Trafalgar, whilst the other, glimpsed between the winding engine house and the left hand chimney, was used for pumping which was carried out using a beam engine. The deputy manager's house can be seen on the left with stacks of timber beyond. The main saw mills for Trafalgar were sited here, all the timber used in the pit being taken through the tunnel. The saw mills burnt down in February 1917 and all the machinery was destroyed. However, they were rebuilt on the same site by November after a temporary building had been erected at Trafalgar.

Collection A. K. Pope

had taken over the Speculation, Rose-in-Hand, Twenty Inches and Trafalgar gales from H. Crawshay and the Foxes Bridge Co. It may have been that this new company was part of the Crawshay empire as, in August 1924, it was reported to Crawshay's shareholders that Trafalgar was to be abandoned. This would have affected 300 employees, but it was said that the blow would be tempered by a long spell of under-employment as latterly only one day a week had been worked.

Nothing appears to have happened immediately as in June 1925 it was stated that due to huge accumulated losses, Trafalgar was likely to close in the near future. On 14th August a report appeared in the *Dean Forest Mercury* that notices to terminate the employment of the workforce would be served the following Monday.

The final details of the closure are uncertain. It seems that the colliery closed the following month, September, the private siding agreement being terminated at the same time. It may have been that pumping continued for a while but was interrupted by the coal strike in 1926, one report stating that upon the conclusion of the strike the workings were found to be flooded. The effects of the concern were sold off by auctions between 1925 and 1927.

There was a later proposal to extend the remaining portion of the Trafalgar siding for the use of Messrs. Forest Products, but nothing came of this.

Unfortunately, no close-up photograph of a Trafalgar wagon has come to light, although a good impression of their appearance can be gained from the views on pages 292 and 293. In addition to the colliery's own wagons, others, such as the two shown here branded as empty to Trafalgar Colliery, would have been found on the regular Southampton and West Country coal trains via the Severn Bridge.

GRC & W Co.

This delightful study remains the only known view of the station before the withdrawal of passenger services. According to former staff, the short wheelbase Midland Railway brake vans, hired from that company for one shilling per day, were more common on the S & W than the familiar GWR 'Toads'.

H. Patterson Rutherford

Looking east through the station, with the Mineral Loop on the right, on 26th March 1948. The loop siding on the Mineral Loop was used for the storage of empties waiting to be taken to Crump Meadow Colliery, whilst the loop opposite the platform, apart from being used by locomotives running round trains, was also used for loaded Crump Meadow wagons awaiting collection. *L. E. Copeland*

DRYBROOK ROAD

Drybrook Road was indeed an obscure and remote location for a railway station, yet, from 1875 when passenger services commenced over the S & W, this was the nearest the service got to Cinderford. It is difficult now to assess whether the station simply formed a convenient terminal at which locomotives could run round to the other end of the train to reverse direction for the run to Lydbrook, or whether it was primarily intended to serve the town of Cinderford. Passenger trains were not allowed to reverse at Serridge Junction, and Drybrook Road, only 1¾ miles further on, was just clear of the long 1 in 40 gradient previously mentioned.

The station, originally to be named Nelson Road and sited on the 'up' side of the Mineral Loop, was instead built on the 'down' side of the line connecting the Mineral Loop with the GWR Forest of Dean branch. This connection was provided when the Mineral Loop was first built. Facilities were basic, a simple Eassie wooden station building and what was presumably a urinal by the same company.

The inspecting officer for the Board of Trade delayed the opening of the line for passenger traffic for one month from 8th June 1875 until certain work had been carried out, but on 11th July G. W. Keeling wrote to Colonel Rich stating 'I am afraid Drybrook Road will not be ready for inspection this week. The signal contractors (Crumlin Viaduct Co.) have not been so prompt as I expected and have not yet fixed the signals and locking gear on that

portion'. Colonel Rich eventually inspected the line north of Serridge Junction on 13th August, and his report concluded 'The signal arrangements require to be completed. Drybrook Station and Junction requires to be signalled as an ordinary Junction. I submit that the line from Serridge Junction to Drybrook Junction cannot be opened for passenger traffic without danger to the public using the same in consequence of the incomplete state of the works.'

Such damning evidence was not confined to this stretch of line alone, the entire Lydney Junction to Lydbrook Junction section being similarly condemned on the same day. This very nearly had unfortunate consequences for the Severn & Wye as, when Keeling wrote to the Board of Trade on 7th September advising that the Lydney to

An unidentified '2021' class pannier tank at Drybrook Road.
Collection Mike Rees

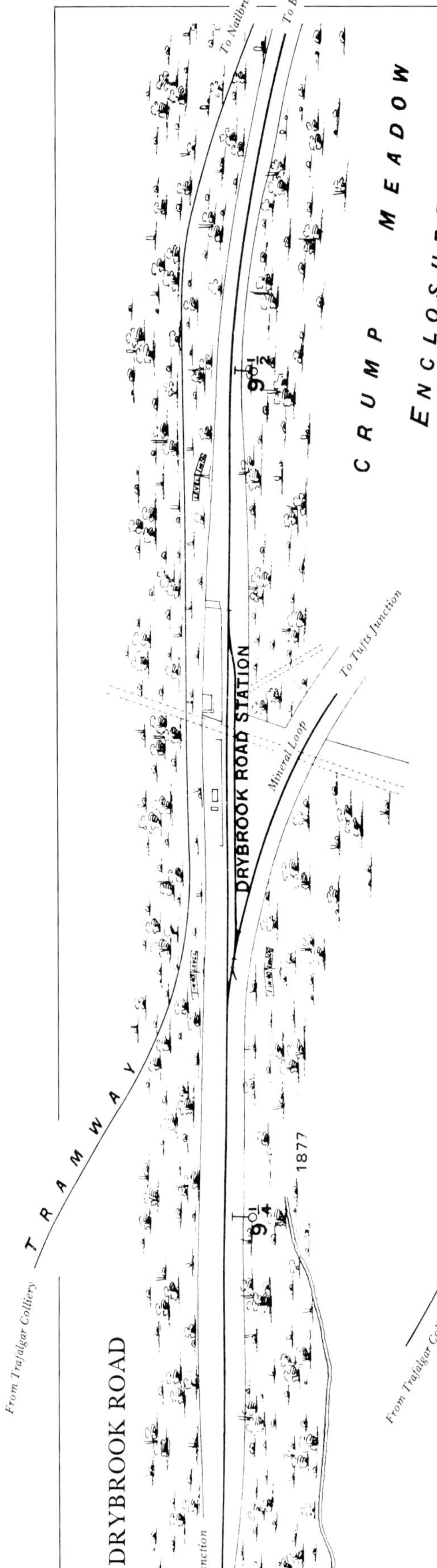

DRYBROOK ROAD

From Trafalgar Colliery

T R A M W A Y

To Nailbridge

To Bilson

C R U M P   M E A D O W   E N C L O S U R E

DRYBROOK ROAD STATION

Mineral Loop

To Tufts Junction

From Lydney Junction

1877

9 1/4

9 1/2

To Nailbridge

To Bilson

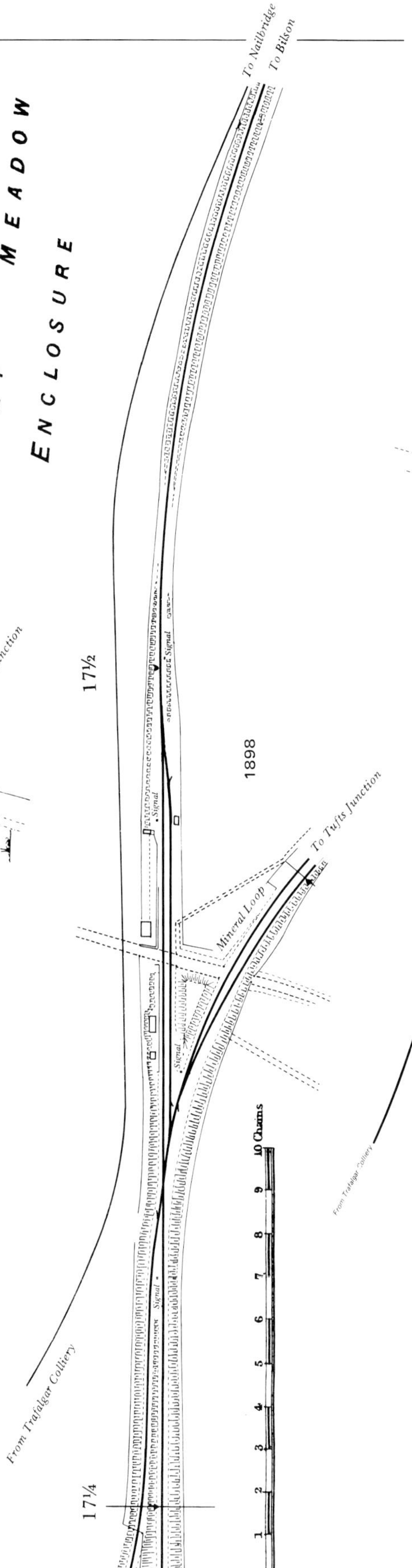

17 1/2

17 1/4

1898

Signal

Signal

Signal

Mineral Loop

To Tufts Junction

From Trafalgar Colliery

From Lydney Junction

100 50 0   1   2   3   4   5   6   7   8   9   10 Chains

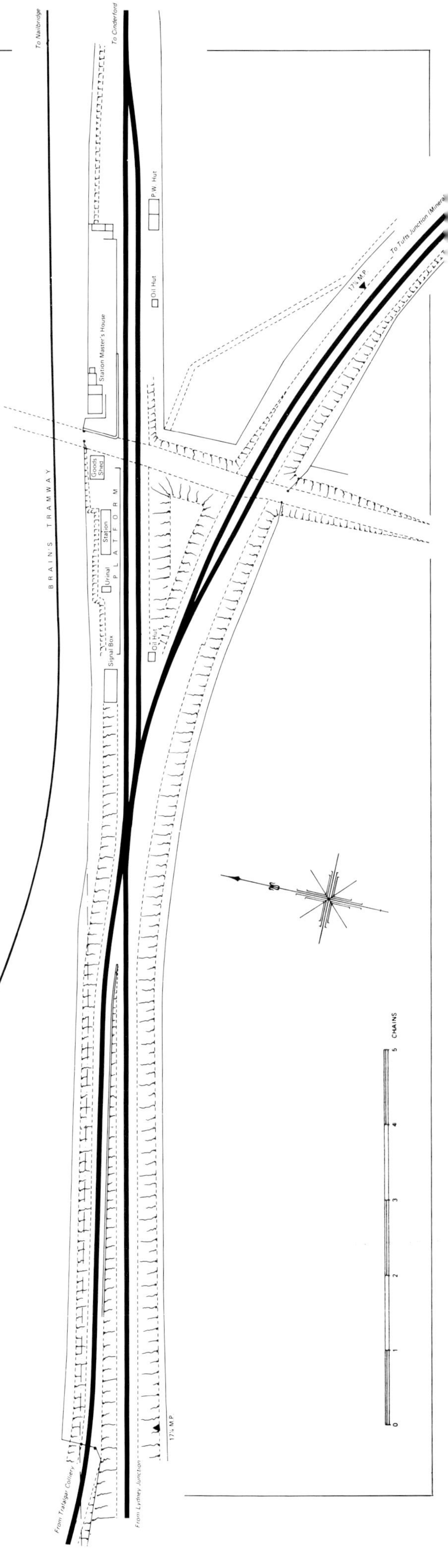

To Nailbridge

To Cinderford

P W Hut

Oil Hut

Station Master's House

Goods Shed

Station

Urinal

P L A T F O R M

Signal Box

Oil Hut

B R A I N ' S   T R A M W A Y

To Tufts Junction Mineral

17 3/4 MP

17 1/2 MP

From Trafalgar Colliery

From Lydney Junction

0   1   2   3   4   5   CHAINS

Lydbrook line works were complete, he omitted to mention that the Serridge Junction to Drybrook Road works were also complete, and the Board of Trade promptly suspended the opening for a further month! On discovering his error, however, Keeling was able to dispatch quickly another letter explaining the mistake, thus enabling the entire line to be inspected and sanctioned by the Board of Trade on 21st September.

Although the original signalling details are unknown, by November 1892 points and signals were controlled from an open lever frame on the platform with 14 levers in use and 2 spare.

Its status as the terminus for Cinderford was reduced in 1876 when a new drop platform was opened on the Bilson branch taking passengers half a mile nearer the town, and when the first Cinderford station was opened beyond that in 1878 there can have been few bookings for Drybrook Road.

The new junction for the revised connection with Trafalgar Colliery, provided in October 1890, almost certainly utilised the double slip which lasted until closure, and a siding provided in 1891 for non-labelled trucks from Trafalgar could well have been the loop siding on the Mineral Loop.

Looking west at the top of the stiff climb from Serridge Junction, featuring the defunct Trafalgar Colliery siding on 6th July 1946.

L. E. Copeland

The junction centred around the double slip giving access to the Mineral Loop, station run round and Trafalgar Colliery Siding, the latter overgrown and long out of use when this picture was taken on 26th March 1948.

L. E. Copeland

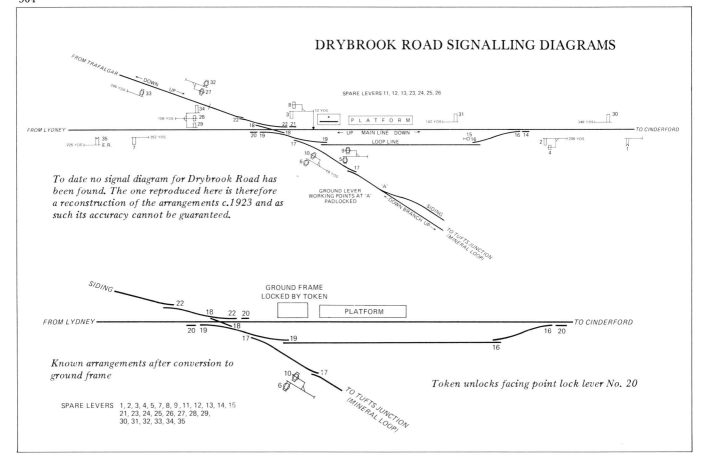

DRYBROOK ROAD SIGNALLING DIAGRAMS

To date no signal diagram for Drybrook Road has been found. The one reproduced here is therefore a reconstruction of the arrangements c.1923 and as such its accuracy cannot be guaranteed.

SPARE LEVERS 11, 12, 13, 23, 24, 25, 26

FROM TRAFALGAR
FROM LYDNEY
TO CINDERFORD
PLATFORM
UP MAIN LINE DOWN
LOOP LINE

GROUND LEVER
WORKING POINTS AT 'A'
PADLOCKED

TO TUFTS JUNCTION
(MINERAL LOOP)

Known arrangements after conversion to ground frame

SIDING
FROM LYDNEY
TO CINDERFORD
GROUND FRAME
LOCKED BY TOKEN
PLATFORM

TO TUFTS JUNCTION
(MINERAL LOOP)

Token unlocks facing point lock lever No. 20

SPARE LEVERS 1, 2, 3, 4, 5, 7, 8, 9, 11, 12, 13, 14, 15
21, 23, 24, 25, 26, 27, 28, 29,
30, 31, 32, 33, 34, 35

The locking room of the GWR signal box had internal dimensions of 26 ft x 10 ft and housed a 35 lever frame. It was supplemented by a lamp hut in 1907 and tablet catching apparatus in 1908, but their location is not known. When this picture was taken on 6th July 1946 the signal box had been relegated to the status of a ground frame with only 8 levers remaining in use.

L. E. Copeland

A closer view of the old Joint Committee notice or timetable board.

L. E. Copeland

The station building at Drybrook Road formerly served the same purpose at Cinderford old station, and is pictured on 26th March 1948. It measured approximately 40 ft x 7 ft 6 ins with a height from floorboards to ceiling of 9 ft. The interior was divided equally into an office with two windows, and waiting room with only one window. When the station was closed in 1943 part of the furniture was sent to Acorn Patch, and later to Swindon. The building was thereafter used by the engineering department for the storage of timber and tools. In later years the office continued to house electric token and occupation key instruments and three telephones.

In November 1895 the Joint Committee agreed to continue the arrangement made between the Severn & Wye and the London and Provincial Automatic Machine Company Limited in 1887 which allowed the latter company to place not more than two 12-slot 'automatic sweetmeat machines' at each station. For this privilege the London and Provincial paid a yearly rental of £25. The machines were to be placed on the platforms 'in as good a position as is reasonably practical' and had to be of a pattern approved by the Joint Committee. To enable the collection of money and for the repair of the machines, a periodical free pass was issued 'from time to time' to enable a representative of the London & Provincial to travel over the line in a third class carriage.

In April 1906 the rental for the machines was reduced from £25 to £15 with the proviso that if the gross receipts exceeded £60 in one year an extra rental of 25% of the excess was to be paid.

In January 1910 it was reported that the Sweetmeat Automatic Delivery Co. Ltd. had taken over the interests of the London and Provincial, and they were given permission 'from time to time' to place additional one-column machines for the sale of Nestlés or Peters' Swiss milk chocolate at the stations. The rental agreement was altered to 10% of the gross receipts from the one column machines and 20% from the others. If in any year the total did not reach £15 the Automatic Delivery Co. were to make up the difference.

The one column Nestlés machine at Drybrook Road is featured in this view, a similar one also being featured on the 'up' platform at Parkend on page 125 of Volume 1. They are still well remembered in the Forest, especially as it was discovered by some that the machine at Drybrook Road would dispense all its contents by the insertion of one penny and the judicious use of a penknife! Quite why a chocolate machine was maintained at such a remote location so long after the station was closed to passengers is far from apparent!

L. E. Copeland

The Forest Ride crossing is frustratingly elusive but is just apparent here.

L. E. Copeland

The increased mineral traffic generated by the new arrangements at Trafalgar must have been in sharp contrast to the meagre trickle of passengers, which can hardly have provided the station staff with a great deal of work. The occasional large load delivered to the station must, therefore, have come as something of a rude awakening to staff more accustomed to dealing with the occasional ticket or two and the odd parcel. One such load, particularly appropriate to the station's isolated situation, was a consignment of 30,000 Norway spruce saplings 12″ to 18″ tall in 315 bundles, plus 750 larger saplings 18″ to 2′ tall, from the Royal Seed Warehouse, Hexham in Northumberland. These were evidently intended for a large replanting scheme and are proof that the trend towards extensive and intrusive pine plantations on England's gentle landscape, which are justifiably so disliked by today's conservationists, was very much in evidence at the turn of the century.

By November 1900 the old timber booking office, evidently not in very good repair, was described as 'worn out'. Consequently the buildings from the 1878 Cinderford station described as being 'in fairly good condition', having become redundant that summer when the new Cinderford Extension Railway was opened, were moved to Drybrook Road. The cost of the replacement was £70 and the work was completed in July 1901. In July the following year a galvanised iron shed was also transferred to Drybrook Road from Bicknor Siding near Lydbrook Junction at an estimated cost of £25. This was probably the building on the 'down' end of the platform labelled on plans as a 'goods shed', but sadly no photographs have been discovered showing this end of the platform, or indeed the passenger entrance or the Forest Ride level crossing. Messrs. Wheeler and Gregory paid rent for the site of a hut here from 9th May 1903 with use of the Committee's siding at Lydney

Junction. This could have been the goods shed but further details are unknown.

The station was completely resignalled in 1904 when, in July, £800 was authorised for work to include a new signal for trains from Trafalgar. A GWR signal box was authorised in November as part of the renewals but as recently as

The station master's house is another elusive feature long since demolished. However, this view, taken after closure, does at least provide a glimpse of two of its elevations. *Roy Denison*

January 1903 the previous 'locking frame' was apparently renewed and two independent discs fixed to catchpoints in the loop, and in January 1904 it was reported that the porter signalman who was 'occupied 10 hours daily in the signal cabin' was to be regraded as signalman.

As Trafalgar Colliery was closed around the time when surviving enginemen started, we know little of operation when Drybrook Road was in full use. In subsequent years most trains were sent along the Mineral Loop from Tufts Junction, those entering from Drybrook Road primarily conveying empties to Crump Meadow Colliery until it closed in 1929. These were drawn up alongside the platform where the locomotive ran round, the brake van was shunted onto the opposite end and, after drawing back clear of the junction, the train was propelled round the Mineral Loop. The empties were left inside the colliery gate. Returning to Drybrook Road, the engine propelled the van along the main line to Crump Meadow Junction to collect any loaded wagons. Access was by means of a small two lever ground frame but certainly in later years there were rarely more than half a dozen wagons. These were sometimes left in the loop opposite the platform at Dry-

brook Road and picked up later when any wagons were collected from Cinderford.

Before the 1929 withdrawal of passenger services, the station was staffed by a station master (who was provided with the adjacent dwelling) and two signalmen, but from 17th May 1927 the line between Serridge and Cinderford Junctions was made one block section with an intermediate token pillar instrument in Drybrook Road office, where the signal box was converted to a ground frame. The staff were withdrawn from 1st March 1928 and a porter appointed in charge, the station coming under the supervision of Cinderford where the box was also closed.

When the ammunition depot was opened at Acorn Patch in March 1943, after the Mineral Loop had been severed through Moseley Tunnel, the junction took on a new importance and, presumably to avoid any hindrance, the station was closed on 30th September that year. However, its renewed importance was short-lived as the track was relaid through Moseley Green tunnel in December 1943, and all traffic to Acorn Patch was subsequently worked via Tufts Junction.

Looking back towards Drybrook Road on 26th March 1948. The start of the 1 in 56 gradient down to Cinderford is particularly noticeable in this view. The signal, although within the station loop at Drybrook Road, was the fixed distant for Cinderford Junction.　*L. E. Copeland*

No photographs have been discovered of Crump Meadow Junction provided in 1882 (inspected 16th October) but this view taken on 27th June 1948 shows the site long after the removal of the track which diverged to the right where the line of the fencing has been interrupted. Laymoor Junction is just discernible beyond.

L. E. Copeland

THE BILSON BRANCH

By the early 1870s the developing town of Cinderford, with its neighbouring collieries and thriving ironworks, was growing in importance as an industrial centre. However, the Severn & Wye was at something of a disadvantage in attempting to tap this promising source of traffic, due to the presence of the Great Western's Forest of Dean Railway which ran to the west of the town.

It is not clear whether the company had any initial interest in reaching Cinderford as when the ¾ mile long mineral-only Bilson Branch opened in 1873 it was simply to exchange traffic with the GWR. It had been authorised in 1869 as a broad gauge branch off the Mineral Loop, but in the event it was constructed to standard gauge, and formed an extension of the main line from Drybrook Road to a triangular junction with the GWR's Churchway branch in the rather bleak Laymoor area to the north-west of Cinderford. Immediately to the west of the junction the railway crossed Brain's tramway on the level, the latter line being used to convey coal from Trafalgar Colliery to interchange sidings at Bilson yard on the GWR Forest of Dean branch.

Whilst the Bilson branch itself was constructed by the Severn & Wye's contractor, J. E. Billups of Cardiff, the connections with the Churchway branch were put in by the Great Western at S & W expense. In May 1873, when work was presumably well advanced, the GWR showed its willingness to make life difficult for its smaller neighbour by asking for an easement fee of £200 in addition to the estimated cost of £250 for constructing the junction. Not to be intimidated, however, the Severn & Wye sought

independent advice and secured a reduction to £150. How-ever, repeated requests that the GWR should also share the cost of construction did not meet with the same success.

Opened for traffic on 15th September 1873, Bilson Junction was in practice worked as part of Bilson yard, of which it formed the northernmost point. The north and south connections were used for traffic received from and passed to the GWR respectively, through running not normally taking place. Only the south connection was provided with a loop at this time, perhaps indicating a relatively higher proportion of outgoing traffic although the high rates imposed by the GWR on Severn & Wye traffic travelling to the east via the junction can have done little to encourage this. This included coal traffic to the south-west and iron ore to the Midlands, via Bullo Pill, and iron ore to local concerns such as Cinderford and Soudley ironworks. The S & W certainly did not appear to be in a hurry to attract traffic away from the GWR initially declining, just after opening, to make a special role for coal to Lydney Harbour from Quidchurch Colliery on the Forest of Dean branch, which at the time travelled via Bullo Pill for as little as 1d per ton less than via Bilson.

The building of the branch spelt the end for the S & W's Churchway branch tramroad, which had previously afforded interchange facilities with the GWR for the ironworks traffic. No longer serving a useful purpose, it lingered on until 1876 when closure was forestalled in the hope that traffic from Hawkwell Colliery might be routed onto the S & W system via the tramroad and thus escape the clutches of the GWR. This evidently did not materialise as on 6th April 1877 the Severn & Wye applied to the Crown for permission to remove the tramplates between Mierystock

CRUMP MEADOW JUNCTION

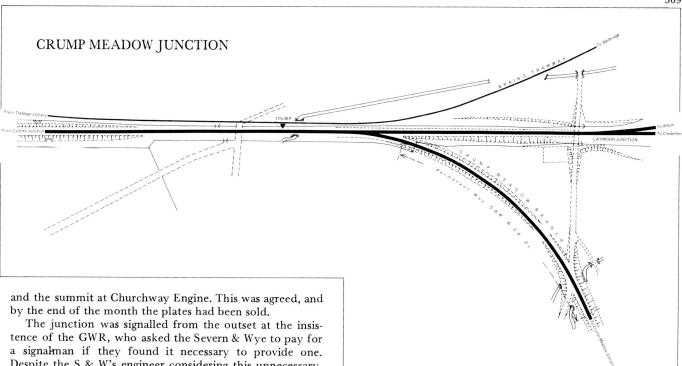

and the summit at Churchway Engine. This was agreed, and by the end of the month the plates had been sold.

The junction was signalled from the outset at the insistence of the GWR, who asked the Severn & Wye to pay for a signalman if they found it necessary to provide one. Despite the S & W's engineer considering this unnecessary, the wily GWR apparently lost no time in installing their man, and the hapless Severn & Wye quickly found themselves being charged the full daily wages and equipment of a 'pointsman' whose attendance was 'little more than nominal', though the Great Western doubtless found plenty of their own work for him to do!

Not surprisingly representations were made to the GWR and after protracted negotiations, during which G. W. Keeling 'travelled with Mr. Grierson and begged him get this matter finally disposed of . . . ', agreement was reached in March 1878 whereby from the date of opening the S & W would pay half the cost of a signalman, whose duties included furnishing the company with a return of traffic exchanged at the junction.

And so, although neither side could have guessed it at the time, an arrangement was made which was to continue down the years and, with a neat twist of poetic justice, rebound on the Great Western in the late 1930s, as will be seen later.

Repairs and maintenance were another early area of contention between the two companies. In February 1873 an agreement was made whereby the Great Western were to carry out all necessary work at the junction and charge the Severn & Wye with the full cost. Before long, however, the S & W apparently felt the charges were excessive and in December 1876 offered to pay a fixed sum of £15 p.a. in lieu of actual costs, this arrangement eventually applying from 1st January 1878.

An interesting episode occurred at Bilson in January 1876 when a mineral train was abandoned by its driver and guard, who went to drink in a nearby public house. They were, however, discovered committing these offences against the company rules and byelaws and duly appeared before the Justices at Littledean petty sessions. Here the guard, one Thomas Worgan, was fined £5 and the driver, James Ellaway, £3, this being a first offence and it 'not appearing expedient to send them to gaol'. They were further disciplined by the Severn & Wye, who dismissed Worgan and demoted Ellaway to the lower rank of drivers!

The Bilson branch was progressively upgraded by the S & W in its attempts to develop passenger traffic, culmi-

nating in the Cinderford extension of 1900, and these developments are described later. The only other significant alteration throughout its existence was the addition, in October 1882, of a siding serving Crump Meadow Colliery. Situated to the west of the tramway crossing, and facing Drybrook Road station, the siding was controlled by a three lever ground frame which operated the points and interlocked with the signals in either direction controlled from the ground frame at Bilson Junction. The siding was used for outgoing loaded wagons, empties being taken into the colliery via the Mineral Loop. It was taken out of use in 1929 when the colliery closed and removed by September 1931.

BILSON PLATFORM

Whatever early success the Bilson branch may have had in capturing Cinderford's industrial output, it was to be several years before its potential to improve the general communications in the area was fully developed.

Although the Severn & Wye introduced passenger services on its main line and principal branches in 1875, the inhabitants of Cinderford found themselves unable to take full advantage of the new means of transport as the S & W service terminated at Drybrook Road station, a mile and a half from the town, and the GWR had also failed to provide a passenger service on the Forest of Dean branch.

The local population were quick to complain to the S & W about the inconvenience of this arrangement and, in July 1876, the company responded by approaching the Board of Trade for permission to extend the passenger service to a temporary 'drop platform' approximately half a mile nearer the town.

The halt, known as Bilson Platform, consisted of a simple wooden platform approximately 80 feet in length with a shelter measuring around 18 feet by 6 feet. It was situated at 9 miles 65 chains on a 1 in 55.8 gradient, approximately 3 chains to the west of the level crossing with the locomotive-worked tramway from Trafalgar Colliery to Bilson Yard. The ultimate intention was to build a permanent station at Bilson Junction itself, but the S & W

Looking back towards Laymoor Junction from the Cinderford extension embankment on 28th September 1947. The site of the temporary Bilson Platform Halt is on the left, just beyond the level crossing, and the formation of Brain's Tramway, which crossed the railway at this point, can clearly be seen to the left of this view.   *L. E. Copeland*

felt unable at the time to make arrangements to convey passengers across the tramway which would satisfy the Board of Trade.

This conclusion no doubt stemmed from a visit by Colonel Rich of the Board of Trade in December of the previous year, when the proposed halt was discussed on the spot, and was amply reinforced by the inspecting officer on 29th July. Colonel Yolland not only stressed the desirability of removing the crossing before the permanent station was built, but also questioned whether it had been sanctioned under the original Act for the building of the branch! However, illegal or not, the crossing ultimately survived until 1890 when the tramway to Bilson Yard closed.

The Severn & Wye intended operating the service with one coach, presumably detached from the 'main line' service at Drybrook Road, where passengers travelling in both directions would be booked. In view of the gradients on the branch Colonel Yolland stipulated that the carriage should be braked or accompanied by a brake van, in case a coupling broke or became unhooked, and in addition obtained an undertaking from the S & W to work the branch with one engine in steam.

There was to be no additional charge (initially at least) for conveying passengers over the extra distance from Drybrook Road, the Severn & Wye hoping instead that the new facilities would bring about an increase in passenger traffic of approximately £5 per month. The company also stationed a man at Bilson Platform, presumably a porter to assist passengers with luggage etc.; this must surely have been one of the most lonely and isolated posts on the railway!

During his inspection Colonel Yolland also drew attention to the need for improved passenger access to the new halt from Cinderford. In fact the S & W had already anticipated this and had written to the Crown on 19th July proposing a

'bridle path roadway' to Bilson Platform from an existing road to Tormentor Colliery on the northern outskirts of the town. This road was described by the Crown as 'a public one, in fact it is a street with a good many houses in it, at least 300 between Tormentor and Woodside', giving an indication of the size of the town at that time. The new road extended from this to cross the GWR's Drybrook and Churchway branches on the level, continuing across the north curve of Bilson Junction before turning south to the new halt.

The Crown granted permission to construct the road on payment of a £1 per annum acknowledgement from the Severn & Wye and on condition that the road was properly metalled and maintained thereafter by the company. However, the S & W's assumption that they would, as a result, have exclusive rights to the new road was quickly proved wrong, the Crown pointing out that the company were simply improving an existing footpath and ride, therefore no such rights could be granted.

Bilson Platform was opened for traffic on 1st September 1876 and was sanctioned by the Board of Trade for one year only, until a permanent station could be built and 'this exceptional method of working be done away with'. Despite a satisfactory level of passenger receipts shortly after opening, the S & W were moved in September 1877 to ask the Board of Trade for an extension of one further year, as the existing arrangements had proved sufficient for the traffic and they had not constructed the new station. The Board of Trade consented to this, but warned that they were not prepared to allow their sanction to continue after this time.

Although shown on Board of Trade plans as a simple platform alongside the running line, the halt is also referred to as a 'drop *siding*' in a Severn & Wye minute book. In addition the 1878 Ordnance Survey shows a short siding on the south side of the line between the platform and the tramway crossing (and also names the halt 'Bilson Road Station'). It is possible that the halt did indeed possess a temporary siding put in to act as a 'catch point' to prevent runaways across the tramway crossing, or used to unload materials in connection with the construction of the permanent station. However, this does not appear in the Board of Trade report of the 1876 inspection and is not mentioned elsewhere in S & W records, so the reference may therefore simply be an ambiguous piece of early terminology. In the absence of any further evidence, the existence of a siding here remains an interesting, but unresolved, mystery.

CINDERFORD 'OLD' STATION

The new station, known simply as Cinderford, was finally opened for public use on 5th August 1878, although not sanctioned by the Board of Trade until the 29th, and was situated on the north curve of Bilson Junction. The decision to site the station no closer to the town than this was almost certainly dictated by the desire, on the part of the S & W, not to incur the expense of crossing the Great Western's Churchway and Drybrook branches.

As the 1878 plan shows, alterations to the layout at the junction were minimal. The new platform was provided with a dead-end road alongside the existing northern spur, with which a connection was made to enable a loco to run round its train. Passenger accommodation once again consisted of an Eassie-style building, but apparently in this case one of 40 feet in length was provided from the outset — perhaps an early indication of the limitations of the original small buildings, which were later highlighted by the extensions at Whitecroft in 1899 and Parkend in 1900.

Facilities for local goods handling do not appear to have been an original feature, and it is possible that part of the station building may have been used initially for goods storage.

Connections to the Great Western were controlled by ground frames on the Churchway branch, as before, while a 6-lever ground frame at the Drybrook Road end of the layout controlled the new pointwork, home and distant signals plus signals protecting the tramway crossing. The tramway was in addition provided with catch points either side of the crossing and these were also controlled from the same ground frame, although the report of a horse killed on the branch in 1886 leaves some doubt as to the effectiveness of this arrangement.

A renewed undertaking to work the branch with one engine in steam also provided for two locos to be coupled together, but it is doubtful if the traffic actually warranted true double-heading and any such working probably served simply to dispose of the locomotives from two separate trains. The branch was later exempted from the provisions of the Regulation of Railways Act of 1889 requiring the introduction of the block system of working, being allowed to continue with one engine in steam as before.

Access to the station was still via the road from Tormentor Colliery and in July 1880 the Severn & Wye arranged for Mr. Smith, proprietor of the Lion Hotel,

Laymoor Junction again, looking towards Cinderford on the same day as the previous view. The crossing in the foreground was part of the road built by the S & W in 1876 to provide passenger access to Cinderford from Bilson Platform, although this particular section may have been part of an original forest track, and the formation on the far side of the track is the course of Brain's Tramway leading to Bilson yard.

L. E. Copeland

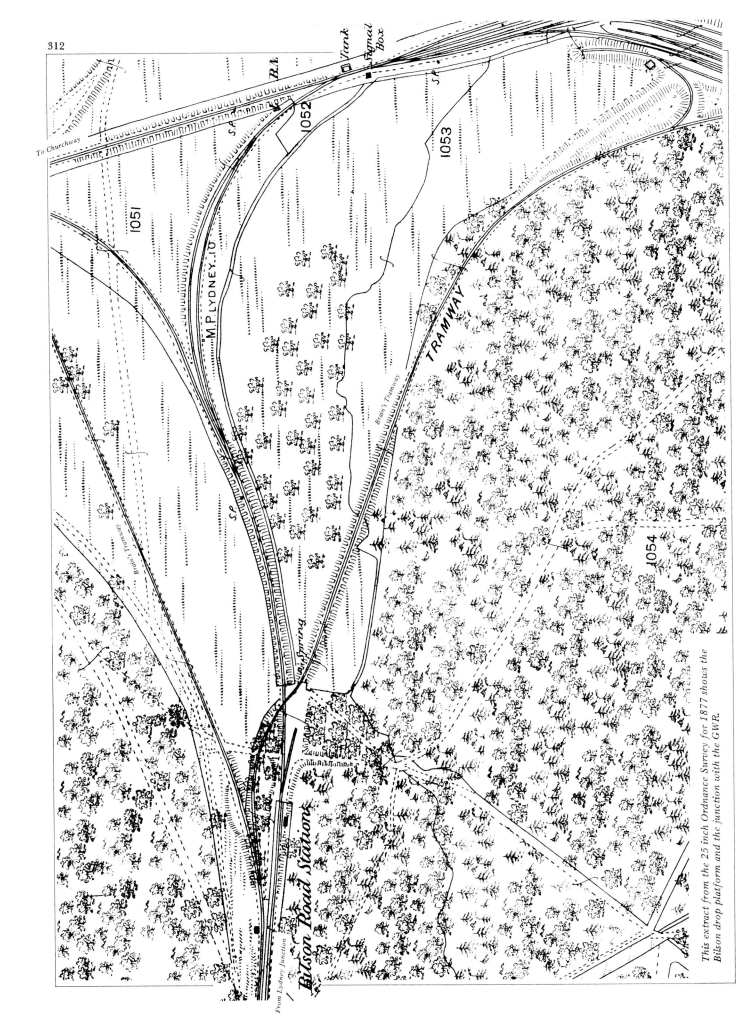

To Churchway

1051

1052

1053

1054

M.P. LYDNEY. 10

TRAMWAY

Brain's Tramway

Tank

Signal Box

B.N.

S.P.

S.P.

S.P.

New Spring

Brain's Tramway

Bilson Road Station

From Lydney Junction

This extract from the 25 inch Ordnance Survey for 1877 shows the Bilson drop platform and the junction with the GWR.

Weeds reclaim the site of Cinderford Old station as it approaches the end of its working life on 28th September 1947. This view shows the connections at the Laymoor Junction end of the station, looking towards the Churchway branch. The wagons in the centre of the view are standing in what was once the platform road, whilst those on the right occupy a siding added to the north loop between 1884 and 1898. The south loop disappears off to the right through the grass towards Bilson Yard. *L. E. Copeland*

Cinderford, to provide a horse-drawn omnibus service to meet every train, with a fare of 6d to any place in the town. In addition, Mr. Smith was to provide a depot in Cinderford for delivering and receiving parcels traffic, the S & W paying him at the rate of 1d on each parcel. However, the omnibus service does not appear to have been an immediate success as, by November of the same year, the Severn & Wye agreed to pay a subsidy of £20 per year to keep it running. This seems to have been enough to secure its continued existence, as passenger timetables up to closure were able to advertise the fact that an omnibus met most trains.

To add to the S & W's problems, the access road's level crossing over the Churchway branch became a source of conflict between the two companies. In May 1880 the Great Western threatened to padlock the gates, stating that there was no right of access over the crossing for S & W passengers. No doubt this was a method of gaining retribution over the Severn & Wye who had begun to take traffic away from their more illustrious neighbour, routing it via the new Severn Bridge. The S & W at once protested to the Crown, but the GWR were still complaining of alleged trespass in August, although the gates remained unlocked. It was probably evident that further conflict would arise and perhaps anticipating this, but more likely due to financial hardship at the time, the S & W made an unsuccessful approach to the Council to take over maintenance of the road up to the edge of the company's property.

Unfortunately, there are no known photographs of the station in the early days, and its appearance and development can therefore only be deduced from official records and track plans. These show that by July 1880 a goods platform had been added inside the south curve. This had a small shed at the western end and a crane mounted in the centre.

In October 1885 permission was granted for Clissold & Sons of Nailsworth to erect stables at the station, and these are believed to be the separate structures as shown at the eastern end of the goods platform on the 1898 plan. This also shows that sidings had been added to both north and south curves, and these are thought to have been added in 1890 when additional sidings were authorised. This may also account for the repositioning of the ground frame on the opposite side of the track. In May of the same year an arrangement was made whereby the Bilson Gas Company were to lay a main to the edge of the station, to which the S & W would connect their own service pipes. It is likely, therefore, that the station lighting was changed from oil to gas at this time, and it is possible that yard lamps may also have been provided though nothing is known of this.

The 1898 plan records one other significant change. A second shed had been added to the eastern end of the goods platform, although it is not known when this was done. One of the two sheds is known to have been brick-built, unlike the Gloucester structures provided elsewhere, but it is not known if this was the later building.

However, by the turn of the century the days of the passenger service to this isolated spot were numbered, and with it those of the junction as a focal point for traffic to and from the town. The building of a new station in Cinderford itself had been included as one of the main conditions of the Severn & Wye's takeover by the GWR and MR in 1894 and this eventually opened for traffic on 2nd July 1900, when the original station reverted to its former

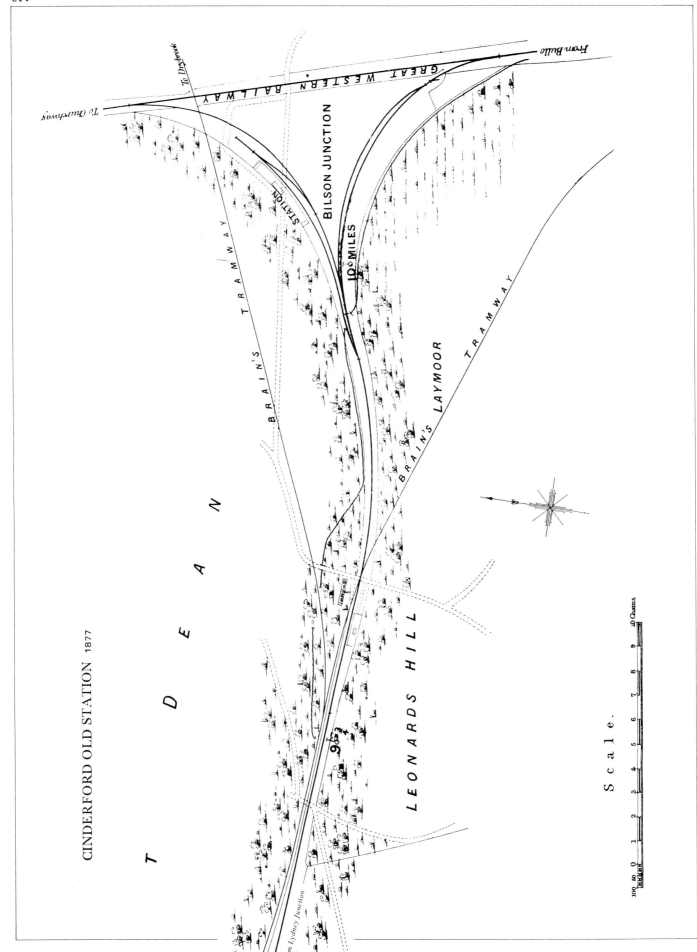

CINDERFORD OLD STATION 1877

Scale.

CINDERFORD OLD STATION 1882

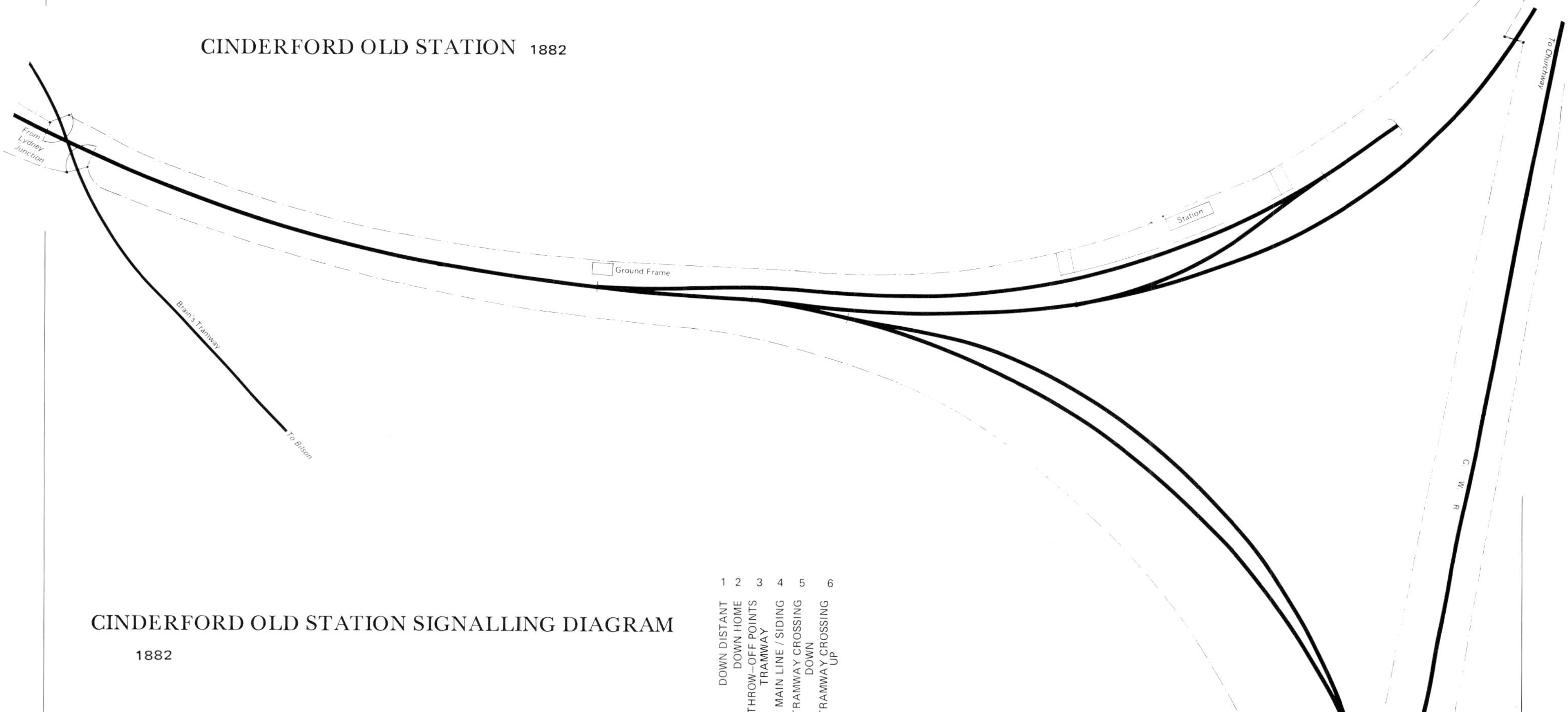

To Churchway

C. W. R

From Bullo

Station

Ground Frame

Brain's Tramway

To Bilson

From Lydney Junction

CINDERFORD OLD STATION SIGNALLING DIAGRAM

1882

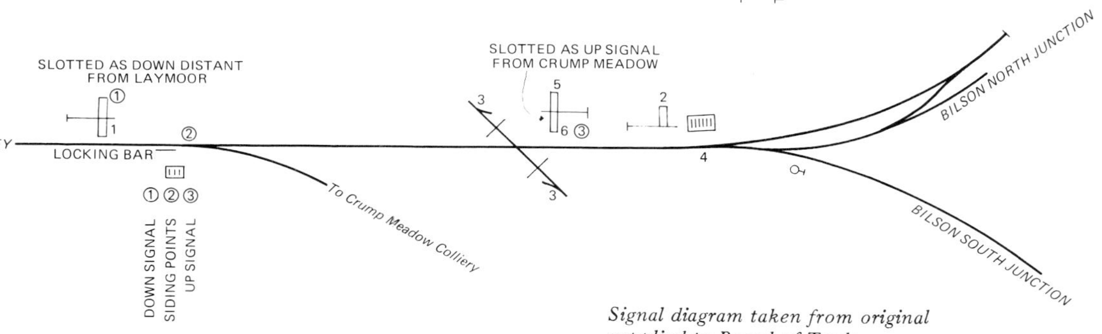

1   DOWN DISTANT
2   DOWN HOME
3   THROW—OFF POINTS
    TRAMWAY
4   MAIN LINE / SIDING
5   TRAMWAY CROSSING
    DOWN
6   TRAMWAY CROSSING
    UP

BILSON NORTH JUNCTION

BILSON SOUTH JUNCTION

SLOTTED AS UP SIGNAL
FROM CRUMP MEADOW

To Crump Meadow Colliery

SLOTTED AS DOWN DISTANT
FROM LAYMOOR

LOCKING BAR

FROM LYDNEY

DOWN SIGNAL   SIDING POINTS   UP SIGNAL

Signal diagram taken from original
supplied to Board of Trade

Just south of the S & W north loop junction on the Churchway branch, this disc and crossbar signal protected the level crossing between the GWR line and the northern branch of Brain's Tramway to the Golden Valley iron mine near Drybrook, and would have been a prominent landmark for weary passengers making the tedious journey to Cinderford Old station from the town. When the tramway closed in 1925 the signal was, surprisingly, left in place and in 1956 its apparent lack of purpose came under official scrutiny. This triggered a series of investigations into the possibility of closing the station completely and removing all trackwork.

L. E. Copeland

role as a mineral-only interchange point, being known thereafter as 'Cinderford Old Station'.

Having waited several years for a new station, it is not surprising that closure of the old station was generally welcomed in the area. Local feelings are probably best expressed by the following 'obituary' in the *Dean Forest Mercury* for 6th July:

> The station at Bilson was quite a mile distant from the Town Hall, even on the very best and sunniest of weathers, and in all other seasons, particularly of course autumn, winter and spring, it was a very long way to Bilson, whether walking or driving. For one thing the track does not appear to have ever been repairable by a public authority, it never having been properly made or dedicated to public use, and therefore even those who have never experienced the jolt in a cart, or the slush whilst 'pedestrianing' it, will readily agree that the sooner something was done to avoid the 'trek' over the Forest to Bilson the better . . .

With the transfer of passenger traffic and station staff to the new Cinderford station the old station slowly settled down into its new, less important, role out of the public eye. It had originally been agreed in 1896 that, on withdrawal of passenger services from Cinderford Old, the station building would remain in place for use by the Crown with the platform being used as a timber loading bank. However, it was subsequently decided, in December 1897, that rather than use the old station building, one of the goods sheds should be retained for Crown use. By a further agreement dated 7th December 1899 the access road from Tormentor Colliery was given up by the S & W, and in October 1900 it was decided to remove the station

building to Drybrook Road where the existing building had become dilapidated. At around the same time the run-round crossover was taken out.

A local person recalls a cattle dock, or similar rail-built structure, at the end of the platform road just prior to the Second World War. This was likely to have been a post-1900 addition as it does not appear on official plans up to that date, but its exact nature must be open to doubt due to the existence of adequate cattle facilities at the new station after this time.

Traffic exchanged with the Churchway branch never amounted to much apart from nominal colliery traffic, and unquestionably the greatest use of the siding accommodation arose from the storage of empty wagons for Trafalgar, Crump Meadow and Foxes Bridge collieries.

Crown traffic probably never amounted to very much either especially as back in 1897 it had been stated that the provision of a siding at the new station would be sufficient. Evidently by December 1908 there was little traffic as the Crown decided to sell the goods shed they were using. An offer of £4 was accepted from a Mr. Harris and the Joint Committee gave him permission to cross the line with his cart to remove the materials. It was then realised that the goods shed was not the Crown's to sell! It still belonged to the railway who ordered that it should remain, but unfortunately Mr. Harris had removed the roof the day before his money was refunded!

Before long the remaining traffic at Cinderford Old was destined to die away almost completely, as coal production in the Forest of Dean slowly declined from a peak in 1898. The reduced demand for coal, becoming more pronounced in the 1920s, led to a general absence of wait order coal and resulted in the closure one by one of the older collieries.

By the early 1930s traffic was rarely exchanged with the Churchway branch. Even the storage of colliery empties became a relatively uncommon occurrence, whilst the opening of Northern United Colliery in 1935 did not generate sufficient new traffic over the S & W to reverse the general trend.

Having survived for some years in an increasingly run down condition, it was perhaps inevitable that the question of removal of the sidings would arise, although it was rather ironic that it should do so as a result of investigations into signalling on the Churchway branch in 1936.

A survey of the points and signals controlled by the Bilson S & W Junction ground frame revealed that the connection between the south loop and the Churchway branch had not been used for traffic for some years. It was

The formation of Brain's Tramway crossing still *in situ* on the north loop on 12th August 1945.

L. E. Copeland

CINDERFORD OLD STATION

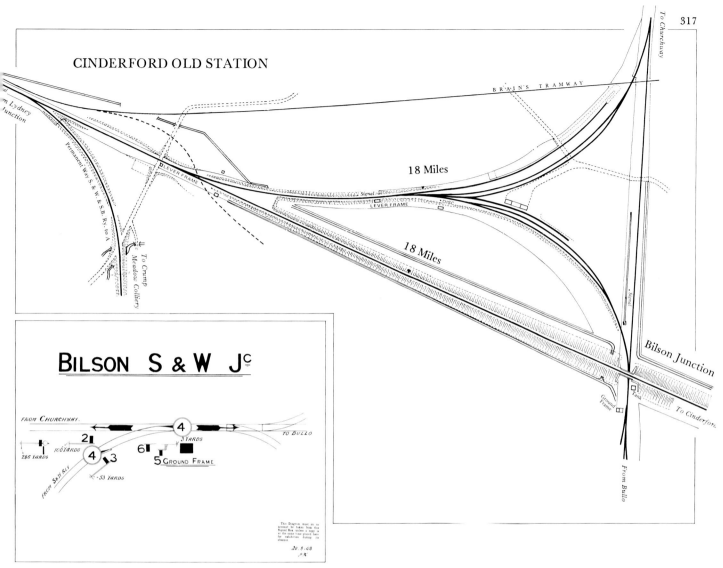

Bilson S & W Junction ground frame, in the centre of this picture taken on 21st June 1932, looking north, controlled the signals and points leading to Cinderford Old station south loop. The Severn & Wye never provided a supply of water for locomotives at the station, their crews being obliged to ask the GWR signalman at Bilson Junction box for permission to use the tank shown here next to the S & W overbridge abutments. Interestingly, the position of the tank appears to have been the same before the Cinderford extension was built, and its presence so close to the bridge must have been an unwelcome complication during construction.

L. E. Copeland

recommended that this should be clipped and spiked for the Churchway branch pending replacement with plain track and removal of the associated signals and ground frame.

Inspector Bracey of Lydney followed this up with a recommendation that the sidings at Cinderford Old should be removed on the grounds that they were unlikely to be required again for the exchange of traffic between the S & W and the Great Western.

Although neither proposal was acted on immediately, further discussions took place during 1937 and in September a notice was actually issued for the south loop connection to be removed in conjunction with relaying work on the Churchway branch, but this was rescinded only two days later.

Further proposals were prepared between October 1937 and February 1938 but again no action was taken, and in April the GWR's chief accountant wrote to no less a person than the general manager, Sir James Milne, pointing

out that the S & W had paid for the connections to be put in and the Joint Committee would receive any savings resulting from their removal. In addition, half the cost of a signalman-porter at Bilson Junction, formerly paid by the S & W, would revert to the GWR if the connections were removed.

The GWR were not keen to have their operating costs rise while half the savings in annual maintenance passed to the LMS via the Joint Committee and, not surprisingly, the chief accountant advised that one connection should be retained in order to preserve the status quo. The porter-signalman's duties were subsequently investigated to determine whether his hours could be reduced if the connections were removed. They could not, it transpiring that the Joint Committee were in effect bearing half the cost of a full-time GWR employee, a situation the S & W were well aware of some 60 years before!

By early 1939 the international situation had worsened and the Amiralty contracted to use Hawthorns Tunnel on

This view was taken from the bridge carrying the Cinderford extension over the junction between the Churchway branch (on the right) and the south loop. Gate posts mark the boundary between Severn & Wye and GWR property, whilst running across the picture, in the middle distance from left to right, can be seen the route of the access road built by the S & W in 1876 to serve Bilson Platform. As part of the general run-down of facilities following closure to passengers, the lease on this road was given up in 1899. However, no arrangements were made for its subsequent upkeep with the result that, by December 1913, a sleeper-built bridge over Cinderford Brook to the east of the station had become dangerously rotten. By 1916 the Crown and East Dean Parish Council had agreed to share the cost of repairs, and the council went as far as making temporary repairs pending the availability locally of suitable sleepers with which to 'make a good job of it', but it is not known whether this work was ever carried out. Ironically, some 30 years later sleepers were in great abundance in the area, being stored alongside the south loop during the 2nd World War as seen here on 12th August 1945. This was part of a policy designed to reduce the risk of loss by fire to Great Western stocks of sleepers and crossing timbers by dispersing these more widely about the system. The 50,000 sleepers stored here necessitated some alterations to the siding accommodation and the provision of a water supply and fire appliances at a total cost of £620, under an agreement approved on 18th February 1942. Although not readily apparent here, it is recalled that the sleepers were of Canadian origin and were stored in stacks arranged so that protruding sleeper ends formed steps to the top, for ease of stacking and removal or possibly to aid access to the centre in the event of a fire. A short wheelbase clerestory camping coach is remembered locally as being stationed in the platform road. Its exact purpose remains a mystery since neither the period nor the location were exactly conducive to happy family holidays, but it may have housed a military guard. The coach was later replaced by a van, of which no details are known. The signals in the foreground are worked from Bilson S & W ground frame, No. 3 on the left and No. 2 on the right. Disc and crossbar No. 1 is in the far distance.

L. E. Copeland

This scene of desolation marks the end of the platform road headshunt, looking north with the engine house of the former Winning or Winner Colliery in the distance alongside the Churchway branch. The view is taken from the point at which the access road crossed the north loop, and the hump to the right of centre marks the position of the former end-loading dock. It was here that, on 2nd October 1892, a train collided with the buffer stop, slightly injuring two passengers. One of the injured parties settled for ten guineas damages plus medical costs but the other, described as 'R. Cohen, Jewish pedlar of Newport', was more enterprising. He demanded £50, was offered £20 and settled for £35 after placing the matter in the hands of his solicitor!   *A. K. Pope*

the Forest of Dean branch for storing explosives. The GWR, with LMS agreement, offered the Admiralty the use of Cinderford Old Station sidings, at a suitable rental, for storing their wagons but the offer was not taken up. As a result new instructions were issued for removal of the sidings, but once again the work was not carried out immediately and by January 1940 wartime pooling of wagons led to the sidings being filled to their maximum capacity of 125 wagons.

Despite the absence of local traffic and the urgent need for materials during the war period, it was decided in April 1940 to retain the siding accommodation for storing pool wagons and to review the situation after six months. However, by June the sidings were empty and Gloucester Division were again pressing for their removal, but with the same lack of success.

In October 1940 the general manager asked for a further recommendation to be made but by this time the sidings were occupied by 84 French Railway vans secured by 12 pool wagons, presumably one at each end of the six sidings, and could not, therefore, be given up. In view of this it was decided to retain the sidings for a further six months and by the end of the year the general manager had agreed to their being used for unloading sleepers which were then stored on the ground alongside.

This, together with the continuing need to store empty pool wagons, was sufficient to defer recovery of the sidings until after the war had ended.

A later view of the station site c.1960 after closure and track removal, showing the stone-built platform face still *in situ*. It is perhaps ironic that, despite the passenger service lasting for only 22 years, the platform face is still visible at the time of writing whereas the later and longer-used successor has been completely obliterated by a modern housing estate.   *A. K. Pope*

THE CINDERFORD EXTENSION c.1900

THE CINDERFORD EXTENSION

A very early photograph of Cinderford station taken from opposite the entrance to the goods yard. A Severn & Wye passenger train is awaiting departure, and the safety valves of the gleaming '2021' class saddle tank are lifting as testimony to the fireman's efforts to prepare his loco for the return journey. The train is made up of Midland vehicles, which were normally used on the Cinderford service, and appears to consist of a bogie brake 3rd, 6-wheel brake 3rd and a 4-wheel full brake. The signal box can be glimpsed through the open goods shed doors and Midland goods vehicles are prominent in the yard. The clean stonework of the goods shed and general absence of vegetation give a slightly bleak 'new' look to the station, in sharp contrast to later views. *A. J. Pope*

Despite the building in 1878 of a permanent station to serve Cinderford, the inhabitants of the town were clearly unimpressed with the new arrangements. The town centre was still almost a mile distant, and the station's location in the marshy Laymoor Quag was far from attractive or convenient for prospective passengers.

As early as August 1884 a meeting of tradesmen at Cinderford Town Hall urged the Severn & Wye to 'bring their Railway Station nearer the town', in return for which an undertaking was made to give as much traffic as possible to the company.

The S & W paid lip service to this request by investigating the legal position and cost of the work involved in making an extension to Cinderford, but presumably the results were not encouraging as no further action was taken.

In November 1885 another approach was made to the S & W, whose general manager met a deputation of the Cinderford Tradesmen's Association which pressed for:

'1.) . . . . extension of the Branch and placing Station nearer Cinderford
2.) Lower Charges on Merchandise
3.) Market Train on Saturdays
4.) Cheaper 3rd Class tickets to Gloucester.'

This time the thorny question of a new station was approached in a somewhat novel manner by the S & W, who investigated the possibility of using the Crump Meadow Colliery's tramroad bridge (Letcher's Bridge) over

the southern end of Bilson Yard in order to gain access to the town, probably seeking to restrict costs. However, it was soon ascertained that the Crown were unlikely to have the power to give the Severn & Wye the right to use the bridge, and there the matter seems to have rested.

In an attempt to placate local feelings, a market train was introduced from the 'old' station in June 1886 (but was taken off in October due to lack of support) and a 2/6d 3rd class fare to Gloucester was proposed, subject to Midland Railway approval.

Nothing further was done by either side for the next few years, which is not surprising in view of the depressed financial state of the S & W, whose receivership must surely have been common knowledge in the area.

In fact the Severn & Wye as an independent concern was able to avoid the burden of building an extension to Cinderford, and it was only when the company was taken over by the GWR and MR in 1894 that the provision of a new station became a reality by being included as one of the main conditions of the Act of Parliament governing the sale. However, local hopes that work would soon commence were sadly misplaced as, in spite of the time limit of four years specified in the Act, it was to be fully six years before the first train entered the new station.

The first act in this long and drawn out saga took place on 14th June 1895 when Messrs. Lambert and Turner, representing the Joint Committee, met a deputation at

Two views of the 'Railway Hotel' under construction at the same time as the station. The prominent earthworks to the left of the building were a favourite vantage point for early photographers, but were less appreciated by townsfolk who quickly coined the sobriquet 'Hotel de Dirt Mound' for the unfinished hostelry. Situated opposite the station entrance, the gates of which can be seen in the upper view, the establishment features prominently in many later views and is today one of the few reminders of the railway's existence. It is possible that these views were taken before the railway fence was set back due to the narrowness of the roadway.

Courtesy Frances Webb

Cinderford and agreement was reached on the site for the new station. This was to be the recreation ground which had formerly been used to hold Cinderford's annual fair, amongst other things, and which was situated in Valley Road approximately ¼ mile to the west of the town centre. Powers were to be sought in the next Parliamentary session to build the extension, which was estimated to cost £12,000 exclusive of land.

It was proposed that the new line would leave the Bilson branch near the site of the former Bilson Platform, continuing straight on across the top end of Bilson Yard and the Drybrook branch on an embankment before turning south into the new station. The area occupied by the extension was estimated to be 14½ acres, and in February 1896 the Great Western's surveyor, W. Williams, reported that the Commissioners of Woods & Forests were willing to accept a rent of £5 per annum for the first two years and £15 per annum for the remainder of a term of 975½ years from 10th October 1895. In addition the Crown were entitled to compensation for timber on the land, and Williams hoped to compensate the recreation ground committee with a payment of approximately £200.

The Crown subsequently received £65 15s 3d for their timber whilst the trustees of the recreation ground, Messrs. Macartney, Colchester Wemyss and Arnold Thomas, received exactly £200, half of which was paid into a trust. This was intended to provide an income for the upkeep of an 'ambulance wagon' belonging to the Forest of Dean Recreative and Medical Aid Association, which was stored in a shed situated on the recreation ground (but presumably not on the portion required for the new station!)

In November 1896 the Great Western's engineer was instructed to prepare the necessary plans for the extension in order that tenders could be invited for the contract. By June of the following year the apparent lack of progress led the Midland to enquire 'whether arrangements are being made for tenders to be invited for carrying out the works?' The GWR's response is not known, but evidently the work involved in surveying the route and preparing drawings was sufficient to occupy the whole of that year, as it was not until 20th January 1898 that the *Dean Forest Guardian* was able to report:

'We are glad to learn that the long looked for extension of the Severn & Wye Joint Railway to the town is about to be undertaken, which news will be most gratifying to the public. Tenders are being asked for in the Contract Journal for the erection of a new covered station and appurtenances and for the extension of the line from Bilson close to the Board School, near which the station will be built. In such a position it will be within a short distance of any part of the town.'

It seems that the invitation to tender had been placed in anticipation of official approval of the plans, as these and the engineer's estimated outlay of £15,562 were not submitted to the Joint Officers (the operating management of the line) until 26th January. Details of the Crown lease had also been finalised by this time and differed somewhat from those originally proposed, being for 16 acres of land at an annual rent of £6 15s 0d for the first two years and £16 15s 0d thereafter, the term remaining unchanged.

Final approval of the plans and estimated costs was granted by the Joint Committee on 2nd February. Tenders were also submitted and opened at the same meeting, these being:

C. Braddock, Manchester	£12,229 10s 4d
D. Pawler, Pershore	£13,280 15s 3d
W. L. Meredith, Gloucester	£14,000 0s 0d
Pauling & Co. Ltd., Westminster	£14,196 7s 0d
Cruwys Hobrough, Gloucester	£15,540 11s 3d

Not surprisingly, Braddock was chosen as the contractor for the Cinderford extension.

News of this appointment was reported with remarkable optimism by another local newspaper, the *Dean Forest Mercury*, which on 25th February stated that the new station '. . . should be open by the end of summer. Passengers will be thankful not to have to wend their weary and dreary way to the old 'shanty' another winter.'

Unfortunately for Cinderford, completion of the station was still almost 2½ years away, the contractor's leisurely progress, amidst growing local cynicism, being well documented in both local papers.

Work in fact commenced fairly promptly, the *Guardian*, appropriately enough on 1st April, reporting:

'Several small gangs of men have started on the extension. After doing a few days' work last week the alarming news spread on Monday that several hands had struck for an advance in wages, and rumour for once proved true. After a little deliberation on the part of the contractor and his men work was resumed as usual on Tuesday . . . . and the work has been watched daily by numerous interested spectators.'

The growing use of heavy machinery at the turn of the century coupled with a relative absence, by today's

A scene of restrained late Victorian revelry at Cinderford's recreation ground, in an age when one dressed up for the fair. Latter day safety inspectors would no doubt be horrified by the flimsy looking forerunner of the 'big wheel', but its occupants appear to be unperturbed as they survey the crowds below from their precarious elevated position. The sands of time were, unfortunately, running out for this genteel activity, as visitors and ride operators alike would soon depart to make way for the town's long awaited railway station. *Collection A. K. Pope*

An interesting photograph taken by a local person in 1900-1, looking towards the rear of the station from Valley Road across the remains of the former recreation ground, which shows evidence of the recent construction work. It is interesting to note that the station nameboard was double-sided and evidently intended to advertise the service to passers-by, as if the sudden appearance here of a large station was not sufficient in itself! The shed behind the station building is not mentioned in official records but a coal store is shown in this position on a later plan. This is actually outside the the boundary fence at this date, and access appears to be via a gate next to the gentlemen's W.C. entrance in the end of the station building. In view of the company's initial reluctance to provide access from Valley Road, it would be interesting to know if unofficial use of this gate contributed towards an early decision to bow to the inevitable and provide a footpath.

Courtesy Frances Webb

standards, of safety measures, meant that construction work was rarely carried out without incident. That the Cinderford extension was no exception is shown by a report of what was possibly the first serious accident, which took place on the morning of Wednesday, 20th July 1898. A mason's labourer was apparently loading a steam crane when a cog broke, presumably in the hoisting mechanism, and a box fell on the unfortunate man, causing a severe scalp wound and 'concussion of the brain'.

The injured man may well have been engaged in loading stone from a newly-opened quarry at Laymoor, near to the old station. This was worked by Braddock from 24th June, and stone for foundations and the backing of walls was obtained from the upper beds. When the lower beds were reached in early September, blue stone of good quality was found and Braddock obtained permission from G. W. Keeling, who was evidently overseeing the construction work, to use this as a facing stone for bridges and culverts, etc. In early October permission was granted for the stone to be used in the construction of the goods shed at the new station.

Once the dry summer had passed, however, the quarry began to make water, due, no doubt, to the marshy nature of the surrounding area. During a break in working of four days the quarry filled with water, and a 6 inch centrifugal pump was installed to empty it. When this was done the pump was removed and a small steam ejector installed in its place. However, this soon failed, and Laymoor Quarry was abandoned around the first week in January 1899.

By spring of that year it must have become apparent that the opening day was still well in the future, as the *Dean Forest Mercury* for 28th April commented:

'Mr. Docwra wanted to know when the new extension railway at Cinderford will be open. It is however not safe to prophesy in such a matter; but at the risk of our reputations as prophets we venture to say it won't be longer than the Whimsey line has been about, and some time next century — the first decade possibly — it may confidently (barring accidents) be expected to be open for traffic, as quite a spurt is being made this week.'

It is not clear whether mention here of the 'Whimsey line' referred to the completed but never opened Mitcheldean Road & Forest of Dean Junction Railway or the Great Western's reluctance to introduce a passenger service on the Forest of Dean branch, narrow tunnels, congestion at Bilson and lack of siding space at Newnham being cited as reasons by the GWR.

By the summer of 1899 it was not only the locals who were becoming concerned by the delay. A letter dated 4th July from Braddock to the GWR's engineer, James Inglis, gives an indication of the state of the works at that time, and reveals that the contractor was by no means solely responsible for the lack of progress:-

'I shall be glad if you will ask Mr. Keeling to send some ballast for station yard and approaches; I have been ready for this some time, and every time it rains the formation wants retrimming, and it is only delaying the completion of the work for no reasonable purpose.

I am also ready for cinder ballast on the bank, if I had this I could put on platelayers at both ends, and join up in the middle, and therefore hasten the completion of the line.

I am very anxious to make a good job and to get the work completed without any further delay, every week's delay meaning a serious loss to me . . . '

Whatever the truth behind the delays, the Joint Committee were doubtless on the receiving end of some very pointed local criticism, and efforts must certainly have been made to counter this with assurances and placatory statements. These were not always well received, as demonstrated by the *Mercury* of 17th November, which stated 'Mr. J. A. Carter [the S & W's traffic manager] expressed the hope that the new station would be opened in December, or at the worst in January. The concensus of opinion was that Mr. Carter must certainly mean December next year.'

In the event the winter of 1899 must have been kind to the contractor, and the *Mercury's* worst fears were not realised as, on 15th June 1900, it was able to report, 'Speaking of railways, we observe that the new station and signals, etc., appear to be pretty well ready for the opening ceremony, if there be one. Hopes are entertained that this may be in July but we have not heard whether the line has been passed by the Board of Trade officials . . . '

In fact an inspection had not yet taken place, but the GWR had by this time advised the Board of Trade of the proposed opening date and had requested either an inspection or provisional sanction to open pending such an inspection. For once the *Mercury* was able to be positive about this in its report of 22nd June, which contains a sad comment on the apathy that seems to have been generated as a result of the long delay:

'. . . definite arrangements are being made for opening the new Cinderford railway and station on July 2nd. Presumably it will be of a very informal character, as nothing appears to be contemplated in the way of a public celebration of the important event. Possibly the hope has been so long deferred that the heart has 'grown sick'. It is a pity that Cinderford traders and others are not associated in some practical way, for with the better conveniences this town and district might be 'exploited' much more than it is at present, to general advantage . . . .'

A week later the opening date was confirmed and it was announced that the first train was to be an excursion to Weston-super-Mare, departing at 7.05 a.m., giving little opportunity for pre-departure festivities!

So it was that the early morning of Monday, 2nd July 1900 witnessed the first train to leave Cinderford's new station, an event long awaited by townsfolk and traders alike in spite of the apparent lack of interest shown in preceding weeks.

Regrettably no photographs appear to have survived of the opening ceremony (or perhaps the photographer overslept!) but the scene is described in the *Dean Forest Mercury* for the following Friday:

'The station and premises are really attractive looking buildings, well finished, nicely painted, and made to look quite smart . . . . platforms decorated with flagettes . . . . The train was made up of a Great Western locomotive and eight carriages, of which two were of eight wheels, four of six wheels, and two of four wheel capacity . . . . all third class . . . . Thomas Norkett driver, Frederick Gilbert fireman, Robert Wilkins guard, ... we record the fact that nobody had the courage to lead off with a single cheer.'

The passenger figures make interesting reading. The train came from Lydney via Lydbrook where 1 got on, 60 at Cinderford, 6 at Drybrook Road, 'too few to mention' at Speech House Road (!), 1 at Parkend, 2 at Whitecroft, 6 at Lydney, 5 at Severn Bridge, 50 at Sharpness, a few at Berkeley and a handful at Berkeley Road Junction where the coaches were attached to the rear of a Cheltenham to Weston-super-Mare excursion.

There were an estimated 250 people on the platform at Cinderford but the opening attracted no 'notables', except for the S & W's Inspector Freeman, and the sentiment was expressed that perhaps the hour was too early for most dignitaries!

The Board of Trade inspection actually took place on 5th July, 3 days after the official opening. It had originally been arranged to take place on 26th June, but the inspecting officer was unexpectedly detained by a House of Lords Committee and had to postpone his visit at short notice. In view of the advanced nature of the arrangements for

A photograph contemporary with the previous view in which the young Frances Webb, dressed in a smock and bonnet, and accompanied by her mother and elder brother, is about to board a train for her first trip to Gloucester. Her mother will undoubtedly have put the day aside for the journey since they will be travelling down to Lydney Junction along the Severn & Wye main line, the opening of the shorter GWR route via Bilson Junction being still some six years away. Their train is made up of Great Western carriages rather than the Midland stock seen in most later views, and suggests that the Joint Committee tried both types at first before deciding on MR vehicles for regular service. The design of the nameboard is worthy of note as it seems to consist of a standard board with cast-iron letters suspended from a highly unusual frame which may well be the contractor's or local carpenter's interpretation of a written specification. *Courtesy Frances Webb*

Two postcard views of Cinderford whose inhabitants were rewarded, after twenty-four frustrating years, with an imposing new station near the town centre. The top view was taken looking south along Church Road, Cinderford, with Victoria Street going off to the right. Prior to 1899 Victoria Street was known as Station Road as it led to the Cinderford goods station at Ruspidge on the GWR Forest of Dean branch. Upon the opening of the 'new' Cinderford station of the S & W, what had previously been known as Bilson Road became Station Street and this can be seen going off to the left in the view below. Although undated, the relatively clean stonework of the memorial to the 'war to end all wars' places the lower view around the early to mid-1920s.

Collection R. How & A. K. Pope

An early postcard view of the station taken from the earthworks next to the 'Railway Hotel'. A '2021' class 0–6–0ST has yet to run round its newly-arrived train and passengers appear to be queueing to give up their tickets at the side entrance. The weighbridge office is prominent next to the goods yard entrance and the cattle dock is visible to the extreme right. The steam lorry is 'Dorothy', a Thornycroft undertype belonging to Francis Wintle's brewery at Mitcheldean. This later passed to Phipps' Brewery at Northampton and is now, fortunately, privately preserved.

Collection A. K. Pope

opening the new line and station, the B.O.T., who were generally well disposed towards new works constructed by the GWR, consented to the start of services pending an inspection.

Major-General Hutchinson's report provides a good overall description of the new extension:

5th July 1900

Sir,

I have the honour to report for the information of the Board of Trade that in compliance with the instructions contained in your minute of the 8th ultimo I have inspected the Cinderford extension of the Severn & Wye & Severn Bridge Joint (Great Western & Midland) Railway.

This extension is a short single line 70.75 chains long. It commences by a junction with the existing joint (single) line from Lydney to an old station for Cinderford.

This line and station are now abandoned for passenger traffic and a new terminal station possessing all needful accommodation has been constructed at the end of the new line.

The steepest gradient has an inclination of 1 in 56 which however extends for only 6 chains from the commencement after which there is a level portion 29 chains long the line then rising on gradients of 1 in 114, 1 in 164 and 1 in 300 towards the terminus.

The sharpest curve has a radius of 15 chains.

The highest embankment and deepest cutting are 24 ft high and 19 ft deep respectively.

The width at formation level is 18 ft. The gauge is 4′ 8½″.

The rails are of steel bull headed in 32 feet lengths weighing 77½ lbs to the yard fished at the joints, the chairs are of cast iron 35¼ lbs each, secured to the sleepers by two ⅞″ bolts.

The sleepers are of creosoted timber 9 ft by 10 ins by 5 ins, the maximum central distance being 2 ft 6½ in.

The rails are secured to the chairs by outside wooden keys.

The ballast is partly broken slag and partly engine ashes and is stated to have a minimum depth of 12 in below the under surface of the sleepers.

The works consist of:-

One overbridge of 28¼ ft span the floor being composed of steel troughing resting on stone abutments.

Three underbridges maximum span 35¼ ft all having steel tops resting on stone abutments.

One 3 ft stone culvert.

These works have been substantially constructed, the masonry being of excellent quality and are standing well. The girders have sufficient strength and give but slight deflection under test.

The fencing is post & wire.

The junction with the old single line is locked with the train tablet in use on the section of single line between Drybrook Road and Cinderford.

At Cinderford Station a new signal cabin containing 16 levers of which 4 are spare has been erected. In this the arrangements are satisfactory and the interlocking correct.

There are no tunnels and no level crossings of any description.

The condition of the new line being satisfactory, I can recommend the Board of Trade to sanction it being used for passenger traffic.

It is being worked by the train tablet and an undertaking as to this mode of working should be supplied.

I observed that the station clock was inside the booking office and requested that it might be moved so as to be visible from the platform generally.

C. S. Hutchinson
Major General

328

Although delays in construction led to a somewhat muted opening ceremony, the station was nevertheless enough of a novelty to attract local attention for some time after this, as evidenced by the two worthies leaning against the boundary fence in the foreground. They are probably hoping to glimpse an arrival, the waiting passengers testifying to the modest success of the service in the early years. Hopes were expressed at the time that the railway might serve to attract visitors from further afield, the *Dean Forest Mercury* for 9th June 1905 reporting 'We are pleased to learn it is the intention of the Midland Railway Company to make Cinderford a tourist centre', a sentiment no doubt received with a wry smile in the undistinguished little town! Although, operationally, the joint nature of the station was never in doubt, the Great Western appearance is undeniable. The excellent quality of this postcard view shows this to have been augmented by the station signs, that to the left of the goods yard entrance clearly displaying a false impression of sole ownership. Also visible, to the left of the station building, is a line of fence posts charting the course of the footpath from Valley Road which the Joint Committee were originally so reluctant to build.

Collection N. Parkhouse

The junction created with the original Bilson branch became known as Laymoor Junction, the new extension thereafter forming the 'main line'. The bridges described by Colonel Hutchinson were, in sequence from the junction, those over the Churchway and Drybrook branches and the course of the Forest of Dean tramway from Bullo Pill, and the bridge carrying Valley Road over the station approaches.

The new station was typically Great Western in appearance, the major structures being built of Forest of Dean stone to standard GWR designs of the period and embellished with the usual 'station furniture' of that company.

Passenger facilities consisted of a single 300 foot long platform and a substantial station building with accommodation comprising a waiting room & booking office, station master's & clerks office, ladies waiting room and lavatories. The full length part-glazed canopy was extended at the buffer-stop end to cover the platform entrance, there being no access into the station building from the rear.

Goods facilities were concentrated on the eastern side of the station where a goods shed road ran parallel to the loco release road, to which it was connected beyond the shed forming a second loop. A pair of mileage sidings with a capacity of 18 wagons each curved beyond this, the furthest being served by a yard crane and a large loading bank with a cattle dock and end loading facilities.

The timber-built signal box was situated opposite the platform end between the goods shed and loco release road,

the signalman being a new appointment in addition to the staff transferred from the old station.

The end result of Braddock's labours was the most substantial station on the Severn & Wye system. This was reflected in the final cost of the extension which exceeded the tender by £3,844 although 40% of this was due to an increase in the price of materials supplied by the company. Braddock also claimed an amount in respect of depreciation on the equipment used during the latter stages of the contract when it overran the envisaged completion date. However, it is recorded that no depreciation was allowed on the locomotive *Glencoe* as, 'owing to sundry repairs effected by the Joint Company the locomotive was in better condition on March 31st [1900] than on November 27th [1899]'! Another locomotive, the ex-S & W *Wye*, was also employed on the extension.

Although a timetable for the inaugural service has not come to light, a 1902 timetable indicates that the passenger service was simply an extension of that to Cinderford Old, the apparent loss of an afternoon train from Lydney to Lydbrook, and the addition of a train in the opposite direction on Thursdays and Saturdays only, being probably no more than a normal seasonal alteration. The 'main line' service had, in fact, reversed at Cinderford rather than Drybrook Road for many years, but the basic mid-week service of four trains per day in each direction could hardly be described as intensive. However, with no competition as yet from the Great Western or omnibuses the Joint

A slightly later postcard view in which the more luxuriant vegetation begins to make the station appear more 'established'. The photographer seems to have captured the attention of a fair sized crowd on the platform, who are no doubt hoping that he will 'get on with it' so that they can board the waiting train! Dating this view raises an interesting question about the accuracy of official records, as the original card is postmarked 1906 whilst the corrugated iron oil store in front of the signal box is recorded as having been provided in July 1907.

Collection N. Parkhouse

A superb close-up of the station building and goods shed taken from another postcard. Both buildings were constructed from Forest of Dean stone laid in random coursed fitted rubble work, but all window cills, door and window arches, eaves courses and chimney caps and bases etc. were of Grinshill white sandstone, as was the station building's splayed plinth course. The station roof was covered with Bangor 'Countess' slates and the canopy was glazed on Rendle's patent 'Invincible' system with ¼ inch rolled ribbed plate glass in metallic channel bars. The station signs were supplied by the Great Western but, of all the notice and poster boards on show, the Midland's are the more prominent. Midland influence is again evident with the presence of the ventilated fruit/milk van, diagram 418 of 1893 standing outside the goods shed. This appears in several early views of the station and was possibly used on regular milk traffic from the Berkeley Vale Dairy at Berkeley station. At this time every effort was made to keep the station neat and tidy and the goods shed doors are seen here receiving a fresh coat of paint. The first mention of any such refurbishment is on 24th January 1905, when a sum of £84 was authorised for repainting the station, and it is possible that this view has captured part of the work being carried out.   *Collection N. Parkhouse*

Committee evidently felt secure enough to adopt a conservative approach when arranging its timetables and, in the November following the opening, an application from the East Dean Rural District Council for the continuation during the winter months of the afternoon passenger train from Lydney to Cinderford was declined. The same body's request for a footpath for passenger access between Valley Road and the new station was also turned down, although a path is shown in later photographs and plans and seems to have been provided in the first few years.

Goods services to the new station would have chiefly consisted of general traffic to and from the town, the more important mineral traffic to the GWR still being routed via Cinderford Old. New traffic was provided by the Nailsworth Brewery Company which had a store site in Cinderford from June 1900, and at the end of the year arranged to erect a storage shed next to the goods shed at the station.

Traffic seems to have developed in a satisfactory manner as, in October 1906, local traders applied to the Joint Committee for the station to be put on the National Telephone Exchange as it was then. The first instrument was apparently located in the signal box, an arrangement which may have appeared logical to the railway company but was quickly found to be inconvenient in practice, a further telephone being authorised for the goods shed office in April of the following year.

1907 also saw the commencement of proceedings which were to bring Great Western trains into Cinderford station, a development which was to have a profound effect, not only on the station and local inhabitants, but on Severn & Wye passenger services as a whole.

On 3rd August that year the GWR introduced a passenger service on the Forest of Dean branch, having constructed a bay platform at Newnham for the purpose and several halts to serve the scattered communities in the eastern valleys.

Ironically the boot was now firmly on the other foot since the Great Western were unable to provide a station on the branch closer to Cinderford than Bilson halt, being obstructed by the new Severn & Wye line. However, having by now a half share in that company, it was natural that the GWR should seek an arrangement whereby it could use the joint station. Not surprisingly, agreement was quickly reached between the two parties and the Great Western was able to advise the Board of Trade of its intentions on the last day of the year.

The connection between the two systems was effected by a new 31 chain single-line loop from Bilson Junction which rose on a 1 in 51 gradient to a junction with the S & W at a point 30 chains from the station. Cinderford Junction was controlled by a new signal box of standard Great Western design, which split the Drybrook Road to Cinderford section in two. Both sections continued to be worked by electric train tablet, as was Bilson loop. The work was carried out by the Joint Committee, but the entire cost of construction was borne by the GWR, who were also responsible for the cost of operating and maintaining the loop and junction.

The new arrangements were inspected by the Board of Trade, who commented that the single junction would be permitted 'under the circumstances' although a double junction was considered more usual, and came into use on Monday, 6th April 1908.

The Great Western was evidently keen to make an impression with its new service, no doubt with an eye to the S & W passenger traffic it hoped to capture, as the inaugural timetable shows. The normal weekday service consisted of five trains in each direction from Drybrook to Newnham plus four from Drybrook to Cinderford, increasing by one Drybrook to Newnham return working plus a single Cinderford to Drybrook working on Thursday and Saturday, with no Sunday service. Trains to and from Newnham called at Cinderford *en route*, reversing down the loop to Bilson Junction before continuing along the branch.

Although steam railmotors had been used experimentally when the Great Western service commenced in 1907, by the time this was extended to Cinderford, auto-trains, using various classes of 0−6−0STs and the occasional 0−4−2T or 2−4−0T with one or two trailer coaches, were normally used.

The extra work involved in dealing with the new 'motor cars' must have become apparent fairly quickly, but the Joint Committee displayed its customary reluctance to increase operating costs by postponing until January 1911 the decision to appoint additional staff. These were two

porters, a signalman, a signal-porter and an adult clerk to replace a lad clerk, and their arrival must have been welcomed with relief by the staff at Cinderford station who had soldiered on for almost three years without assistance.

For use of the Severn & Wye line between Cinderford Junction and the station, the Joint Committee was credited with a one mile proportion of gross receipts from traffic carried in Great Western trains. In addition, under the new arrangements the working expenses of the station, including signalling and maintenance, were divided between the Joint Committee and the GWR in the proportion that their trains used the station. For this purpose two one-coach auto-trains were considered to be equivalent to one Severn & Wye train.

The station master at Cinderford was instructed to be completely impartial when dealing with the respective passenger services, and wore a cap lettered 'Station Master' with no company insignia. However, this attempt at fair play could not disguise the fact that the Great Western now provided the shortest route and journey time to Gloucester, a point which was not lost on prospective passengers.

GWR goods traffic did not use the new loop for several years, being dealt with at Whimsey goods station to the

A fine postcard view taken, unusually, from the yard throat. Features worthy of note are the new brewery store in front of the goods shed, with (empty!) barrels stacked outside, the signalman's tiny fenced garden complete with small tree, and the horseshoe over the signal box door. The wooden structure next to the station building is interesting as it does not appear in other photographs, but it is believed to be the linemen's hut authorised in January 1912, at a cost of £45, when the duties of the three linemen, formerly responsible for the Great Western's section of the S & W north of Coleford Junction, were amalgamated and concentrated at Cinderford. The shape of this structure is very much like an Eassie/Gloucester building and it is intriguing to speculate that it just might have been one of the goods sheds from Cinderford Old Station transferred here subsequent to closure, but unfortunately there is no evidence for this. The more substantial building on the right is believed to be the carpenters' shop, authorised in July 1907 at an estimated cost of £40. In January 1907 a further £35 17s 6d was reported as having been spent on the erection of this structure, and an official plan of around this date carries a note indicating that it was moved to the position shown here, but nothing is known of an earlier location. The gradient post in the foreground marks the point at which the 1 in 164 rising gradient from Cinderford Junction eases to 1 in 300. *Collection N. Parkhouse*

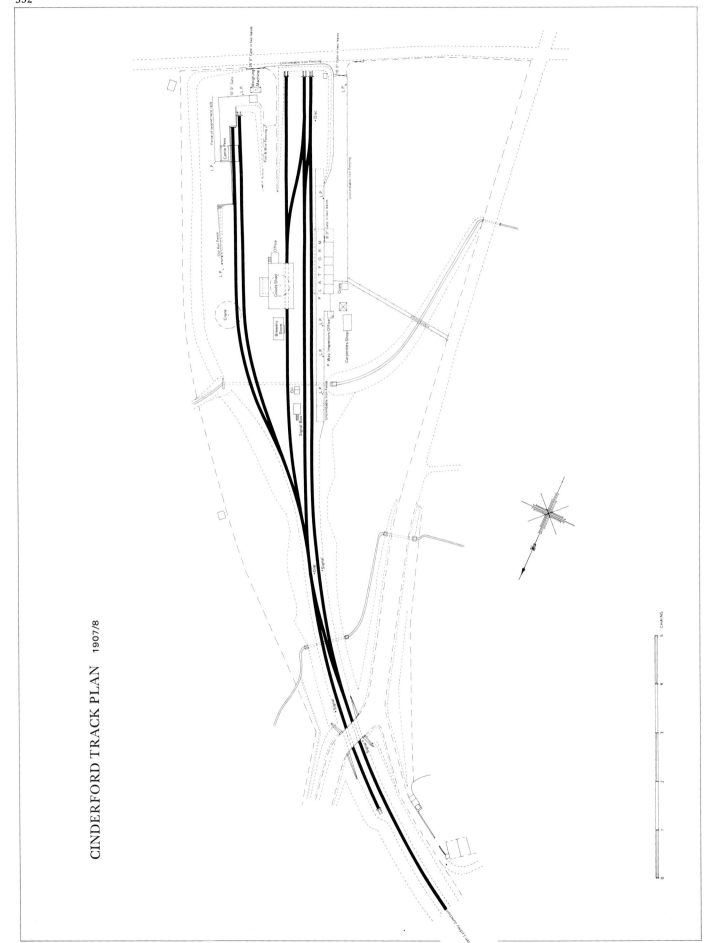

CINDERFORD TRACK PLAN 1907/8

Another early view taken from the other side of Station Road with a '2021' class saddle tank and two Midland bogie carriages forming a newly arrived Severn & Wye train. Prominent in this view is the weighbridge office, constructed in red brick with blue brick window arches and plinth course and a slate roof. This is also one of the best early views of the goods yard and shows the loading bank and cattle dock to the extreme right and, in the distance, the wooden framed loading gauge in its original position. *Collection John Rodway*

A fascinating postcard view of around 1910 which is the only photographic record of the Severn & Wye goods service at Cinderford. This is being shunted by another of the ubiquitous '2021s', whilst its hired Midland brake van stands on the goods shed road beneath the repositioned loading gauge. The loading bank is again visible in the distance and the 5-ton crane can be seen opposite the loco. Despite the action taking place behind him, the signalman is content to enjoy the view from the open window at the front of his box, the deep shadows testifying to the fact that he is probably warming himself in the sunshine. *Lens of Sutton*

north of the town. Parcels traffic was also dealt with at Whimsey initially, although occasional traffic was handled at Cinderford at the rate of ¼d per newspaper parcel, ½d per parcel and 6d per loaded vehicle. From 1st March 1914, however, all local parcels were dealt with at Cinderford at these rates, and a commuted charge of £4 10s per annum was paid to the Joint Committee for parcels traffic to and from Whimsey and beyond which was carried in and out of the station *en route.*

A pattern of services had thus been established which was to continue with little alteration for just over twenty years. The smart Midland suburban carriages of the Severn & Wye provided an interesting comparison both in accommodation and colour to the more modern Great Western auto-trailers with their open saloons, although the adoption

by the latter company of crimson lake livery for carriages between 1912 and 1922 must have set locals wondering whether an insidious form of standardisation had crept in unannounced!

In the aftermath of the Great War, however, the return to normality was accompanied by many changes to the fabric of everyday life, not the least of which was the increasingly widespread use of motor transport, arising initially from the availability of large numbers of surplus army vehicles. This was the case in the Forest of Dean as elsewhere in the country and, together with the growing number of Great Western trains from Cinderford running through to Gloucester from 1913 onwards, it brought about a gradual, but irreversible, decline in Severn & Wye passenger receipts. By the late 1920s traffic had declined

CINDERFORD SIGNAL BOX DIAGRAM

FROM LYDNEY

This poor quality undated print is the only known close-up photograph of Cinderford signal box, and what a mystery it is! The box is a standard Great Western timber structure to a design introduced in late 1899 for locations where a box smaller than 17 ft x 12 ft was required. However, these wooden boxes did not normally have finials (it was only the fourth such box to be constructed) and the 6-light windows are nothing like the standard windows of the period. The explanation for this may lay in the fact that the GWR's signal department at Reading was instructed to provide the box in April 1900, only 3 months before the station opened. The box may possibly have been hastily put together using some odd windows which were in stock, or alternatively, perhaps, this design may have been easier and quicker to fabricate than the standard 5-light pattern.

The paint scheme is even more difficult to explain. The overall impression is of a basically one-colour livery, but the original print hints at lighter barge boards and corner posts, whilst the window frames are certainly white. The upper and lower halves of the timber cladding are undoubtedly the same colour, and there is no rational explanation for this. Since paints were mixed on the spot, a 'wartime utility' paint scheme would seem to offer more by way of camouflage than economy, and there is in any case no written evidence of such a practice to support this theory. However, there is no other convincing explanation, except for the remote possibility of a short-lived local style, and the appearance of the standard GWR light and dark stone livery in all other photographs of the box only serves to deepen the mystery.

Cinderford box was recorded as having locking room measurements of 15 ft x 10 ft x 7 ft to the operating floor, and had 12 levers in use and 4 spare at the time of opening in July 1900. It controlled the signals at the approaches to the station, plus the loco release crossovers, until taken out of use on 17th May 1927 when the S & W passenger service ceased and new ground frames were installed. Two staff were reported as leaving Cinderford at that time. Signalman Jack Cook went to Bilson Junction and later to Bullo Pill and one F. H. Keep, grade unknown, went to Stroud as a 'motor car' attendant. However, the staff shown in this view cannot be positively identified as these individuals.

The box was not demolished immediately, but remained in place for a further quarter century, presumably as a store.

Collection Reg Vaughan

This enlargement from the postcard view on page 326 is included as it is the only available view of the original signals situated either side of the Valley Road overbridge. Visible beyond the bridge to the left is the Cinderford station home signal with the subsidiary arm controlling access to the goods yard out of sight below this. To the right on this side of the bridge is a post bearing Cinderford Junction home and fixed distant arms, the latter painted in the then current style of red with a white chevron, plus a subsidiary arm with large 'S' controlling shunting movements on the running line. Closest to the platform is the starting signal. Valley Road, as one of Cinderford's main thoroughfares, was seriously affected by the lengthy construction works prior to opening. Local feelings doubtless ran high, the *Dean Forest Mercury* for 3rd March 1899 reporting: 'The awful condition of the lower Cinderford road since the new railway contractors have held possession, and diverted the road temporarily, is well known. The clerk reported that G. W. Keeling and Braddock had met the council's surveyor when it was agreed that the contractor should turn the traffic over the new road by means of a wood bridge which will later be replaced by a permanent iron structure.' The permanent structure was the plate girder bridge seen here, which was altered in later years with replacement brick parapets as seen on page 345.

Collection N. Parkhouse

Cinderford goods staff pictured outside the goods shed, their uniform caps bearing the distinctive 'GW & MID' badges which date this view as no later than the early 1920s. At this time the staff evidently had sufficient pride in their work to cultivate a flower border along the base of the wall facing the station building, a feature sadly lacking in later views.

Collection A. K. Pope

to the point where economies were necessary, and the end of the S & W passenger service was in sight.

The first steps in the Joint Committee's search for savings were taken on 28th April 1927 when 'with the view to effecting economy in the working of the line between Cinderford Station and Cinderford Junction it was recommended that the station signal box be removed and the section worked by one engine in steam'. No time was lost in putting the recommendation into force, and Cinderford signal box was taken out of use on Tuesday, 17th May 1927, and replaced by new ground frames at each end of the station. These were locked by a key on the wooden train staff which was introduced between the station and Cinderford Junction. Trains starting from Cinderford station after this date had to whistle to attract the attention of the Junction box in order to be signalled forward.

At the same time, as previously mentioned, the line between Cinderford and Serridge Junctions was made one block section, and the electric train token replaced the tablet instruments previously in use. The key token, like the tablet it replaced, unlocked the ground frames at Crump Meadow siding and Laymoor Junction.

By September 1928 the Severn & Wye weekday passenger service consisted of two through workings from Berkeley Road to Lydbrook Junction via Cinderford, and one from Lydney Junction, plus return workings from Lydney Junction and Berkeley Road to Cinderford. The Saturday service substituted a return working to Lydbrook Junction for that to Lydney Junction and added a further return working from Lydney Junction to Lydbrook Junction via Cinderford. However, it is likely that by this date many of these trains were running virtually empty, whereas the more intensive Great Western service continued to enjoy greater success in attracting passengers.

The last Severn & Wye passenger train north of Lydney Town eventually ran on 6th July 1929. Although protests were made elsewhere in the Forest, the occasion seems to have warranted little or no comment from the townspeople of Cinderford, who evidently felt that the service which was so eagerly sought after by their Victorian predecessors had outlived its usefulness in the 'modern age'.

The line from Lydney remained open for the dwindling number of Severn & Wye goods trains, and on 26th June 1930 the motor economic system of maintenance was introduced in order to effect further economies on the section north of Coleford Junction. The original six permanent way lengths were re-allocated to two gangs of ten men each based at Coleford Junction and Cinderford Junction where various huts were provided to house the motorised trolleys and other equipment. This enabled the Great Western to save a total of 4 gangers and 4 sub-gangers for an outlay of £2,075 in providing the trolleys, trailers, huts, etc.

The Joint Committee's horse dray pictured outside the Lion Hotel from where the original omnibus service to Cinderford Old station operated. The inscription 'GW & MR' which is just discernible on the tailboard again dates this view as no later than the early 1920s but it is not known whether the dray seen here was supplied to an agent or operated by the Joint Committee itself. The first cartage agent at Cinderford was a Mr. Powell, who was succeeded by Messrs. R. T. Smith & Co. on 1st January 1903. Smith's were still in business in October 1921 when they successfully applied for an increased rate of payment in view of rising costs and the 'hilly nature of the district', which necessitated the use of two horses for the work and occasional detours to avoid the steep climb up Station Street when carrying heavy loads. After this date details were less clear, but it is apparent that by the time of the Second World War, cartage was performed with a motor lorry provided by the Joint Committee, who may possibly have taken over responsibility for the service by that time.   *Collection A. K. Pope*

Looking towards the station from the Valley Road overbridge on 21st June 1932 with the goods yard headshunt still intact. By this date the signal box had been taken out of use and the signal seen here was the fixed distant for Cinderford Junction.   *L. E. Copeland*

Withdrawal of the S & W trains left the Great Western service, a relative newcomer to the scene, as the last remaining passenger service to run into the heart of the Forest. As such, the Cinderford to Gloucester service appeared fairly secure for some time to come. However, the same could not be said of the uneconomic section north of Cinderford, and the last passenger train to Drybrook ran on 5th July 1930.

The remaining auto-trains to Gloucester soldiered on in the face of growing competition from bus services. A minor triumph for the omnibus faction occurred on 11th August 1930 when arrangements were made for the Bristol Tramways & Carriage Co. Ltd. to stand a bus on the forecourt between 9 p.m. and 9 a.m. 'in such a position as directed by the Station Master'.

In retrospect one wonders whether the Joint Committee were entirely wise in allowing an overnight parking arrangement so well suited to advertising the bus service to rail passengers. For the time being, however, the branch service continued to provide its passengers with the opportunity to enjoy the scenery of the pleasant, wooded valleys south of Cinderford on its circuitous journey to Gloucester, surely a bonus for all save those in a hurry.

Locos were supplied by Lydney after the Great Western shed at Bullo Pill closed on 23rd March 1931. In June 1933 the first of the new 48XX class 0—4—2Ts to come to the area was allocated to Lydney, and this class monopolised the Cinderford auto service almost to the end.

From 1930 onwards a number of abortive proposals were made to resurrect a passenger service on various parts of the Severn & Wye system north of Lydney. The last of these, and perhaps the closest to becoming a reality, was the proposed introduction in 1936 of a Saturdays-only service between Cinderford and Upper Lydbrook using auto-trains. A test on 27th February was successful, but the scheme was abandoned as it would have required alterations to goods and mineral services.

The years following World War II saw the advent of Nationalization, which placed Cinderford under the control of British Railways Western Region. The decline in traffic became more pronounced, and the first casualty was the Severn & Wye goods service. In later years a locomotive and brake van had set off more in the hope that the expectation of obtaining traffic and finally, from 25th July 1949, the service was withdrawn between Serridge Junction and Cinderford Junction.

The track was broken at these points on 31st December 1951, isolating Cinderford station from the rest of the S & W system. Cinderford Junction signal box was closed and the line between the station and Bilson Junction was made one block section.

One of Cinderford Junction's motorized permanent way trolleys pictured on the goods shed road in the early 1930s. Comparison with the head-on view of the same vehicle on page 28 of Vol. 1 reveals that its proportions are similar to those of early broad gauge horseboxes, being considerably wider than it is long and evidently intended for one or two man use.

Collection A. K. Pope

A PICTORIAL JOURNEY ALONG THE CINDERFORD EXTENSION

To complement the history of the most recent of Cinderford's three stations, this pictorial journey along the Cinderford extension serves to portray the character and setting of this short but interesting section of line in its final years.

Laymoor Junction, where the Cinderford Extension Railway, which ran straight on and over the GWR F.O.D. branch, joined the old S & W main line to the original Cinderford station and exchange sidings. This view of the junction, on 21st June 1932, looking down the track in the Cinderford direction, shows clearly why this stretch was known locally as the 'straight rail'. The connection with the original Bilson branch was laid in by the Severn & Wye when work commenced on the new extension, the contractor being required to construct any temporary sidings needed to receive materials supplied by the Joint Committee.

L. E. Copeland

Looking east along the Cinderford extension over the GWR's Churchway branch towards the terminus on 27th June 1948. Bilson S & W ground frame (GWR) can be seen on the lower level and Cinderford Junction home signals are visible in the distance.   *L. E. Copeland*

The bleak and uninviting location of Cinderford Old station is clearly portrayed in this view, dated 26th March 1948, looking north from the bridge featured above. Although the track layout shows signs of wartime alterations, the triangular layout of the junction can be clearly seen.

L. E. Copeland

Looking back along the Cinderford extension embankment towards the Churchway branch underbridge on 26th March 1948. This view also shows how the extension has effectively cut off the old station from the rest of Bilson Green and its busy railway complex. Passengers during the early days would have had a relatively unobstructed view of the bustle of activity at Bilson Junction as a questionable compensation for their tedious journey from the town.   *L. E. Copeland*

Looking towards Drybrook Road from the platform of the bracket signal next to Cinderford Junction signal box on 6th October 1946. Bilson loop curves away to the left and the Great Western line to Drybrook is visible between this and the wagons standing at the top end of Bilson Yard. The course of the Forest of Dean tramroad to Whimsey can be seen cutting through both embankments beyond the signals. Although almost certainly out of use when the Cinderford extension was built, it appears likely that complications over formal abandonment of the tramroad may have led to the provision of underbridges in order to preserve the trackbed intact.   *L. E. Copeland*

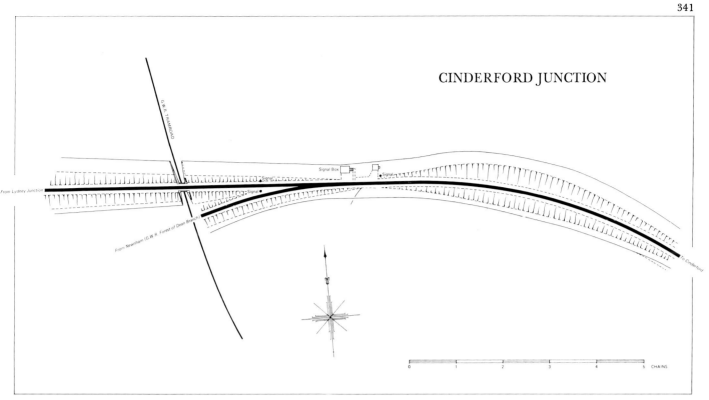

CINDERFORD JUNCTION

A view of Cinderford Junction signal box with the signalman, George Whittington, standing at the top of the steps. Activity at the box was probably never very great and the story is told of the signalman who was promoted to Woolaston box on the Gloucester-Chepstow main line and after a couple of weeks wished to return to Cinderford as trains went past his new box too fast!

Collection A. K. Pope

CINDERFORD JUNCTION SIGNAL BOX DIAGRAM

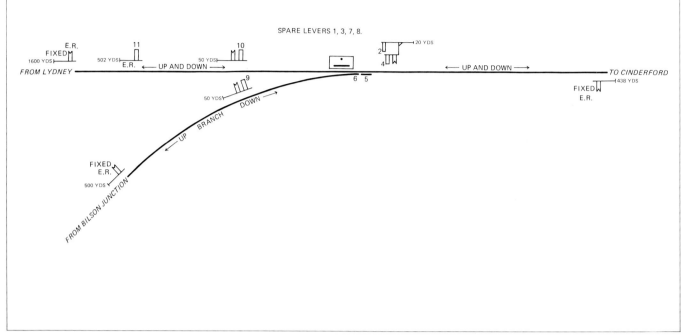

SPARE LEVERS 1, 3, 7, 8.

E.R.
FIXED   11   10   20 YDS

1600 YDS   502 YDS   50 YDS   2

FROM LYDNEY   E.R.   ← UP AND DOWN →   4   ← UP AND DOWN →   TO CINDERFORD

6   5   438 YDS

9   FIXED

50 YDS   E.R.

← UP   BRANCH   DOWN →

FIXED
E.R.

500 YDS

FROM BILSON JUNCTION

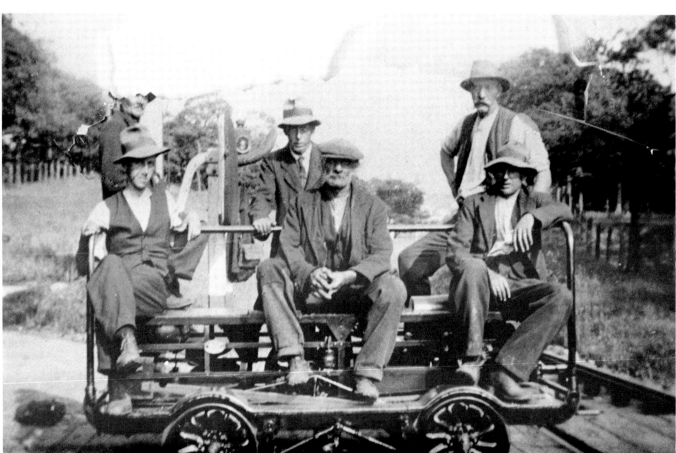

A damaged but nevertheless characterful study of six members of Cinderford Junction's permanent way gang pictured aboard one of the larger motorised trolleys.

Collection A. K. Pope

Cinderford Junction again, looking up the embankment from the trackbed of the Forest of Dean tramroad on 28th September 1946. The closest signals are both Cinderford Junction down homes and Cinderford station fixed distants for the Severn & Wye line and the Bilson loop respectively, a Great Western train being signalled from the loop line. *L. E. Copeland*

A final view of Cinderford Junction on 6th October 1946 from the top of the Bilson loop signal, showing, beyond the box, the huts housing the permanent way gang's motor trolley and other equipment, and the bracket signal consisting of S & W and Bilson loop up homes and Bilson Junction fixed distant. After Cinderford station signal box was taken out of use in 1927, the token exchanging apparatus at the junction fell out of use because the wooden train staff used on the Cinderford Junction-Cinderford Station section could not be set down on the apparatus and had to be exchanged by hand. *L. E. Copeland*

Sunlight casts deep shadows across the shallow cutting leading to Cinderford Junction in this view from the Valley Road overbridge in later years.

Keith Allford

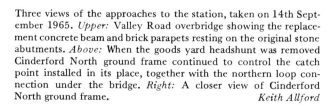

Three views of the approaches to the station, taken on 14th September 1965. *Upper:* Valley Road overbridge showing the replacement concrete beam and brick parapets resting on the original stone abutments. *Above:* When the goods yard headshunt was removed Cinderford North ground frame continued to control the catch point installed in its place, together with the northern loop connection under the bridge. *Right:* A closer view of Cinderford North ground frame. *Keith Allford*

346

Another view of the station from the Valley Road overbridge on 28th September 1946 which provides an interesting comparison with that on page 337. The most obvious difference is the absence of the goods yard headshunt which was described as being redundant when its removal was approved on 9th January 1941.

L. E. Copeland

A 1940s view showing one of the Great Western auto-trains which by that time formed the only passenger service into the station. A porter stands next to a large stack of boxes on the otherwise deserted platform and the shabby, peeling exterior of the signal box adds to a general impression of the beginnings of decline. *Lens of Sutton*

Another of the familiar motor trains is seen here on 30th June 1955, the viewpoint revealing that much of the platform surface has been altered from paving to gravel. The gas lamps have also changed, this possibly having taken place in 1922 when the original upright burners were replaced by incandescent burners in order to provide better lighting. The brick-built structure nestling under the trees in the centre of this view replaced the former linemen's hut seen on page 331. It is not known when the new structure was built, or what purpose it originally served, but it was latterly used as the station master's office. *S. Fletcher*

A '14XX' class 0–4–2T and auto-trailer await the appearance of passengers in the spring sunshine on 17th May 1948, and an LNER box van with exterior sliding shutters sits outside the goods shed doors which, unusually, are closed on this occasion. The recent nationalisation of the country's railway system has had little effect as yet on this tranquil scene. *L. E. Copeland*

Left: The gas meter house sits unobtrusively in the shadows beneath the trees next to the station entrance. *Right:* A closer view of Cinderford South ground frame which can be seen on the left in the view above. This and its opposite number at the northern end of the station, controlled both ends of the loco release road and came into use on 17th May 1927 when Cinderford box was closed, the south ground frame being taken out of use in 1961 when the loco release crossover was removed. *L. E. Copeland*

A pannier-hauled autotrain features in an atmospheric scene beneath the platform canopy on a rainy day in the 1950s, which must surely evoke strong memories in those who once used the passenger service. Those who can, may remember the station's chocolate machine which, like its counterpart at Drybrook Road, was a great attraction for local youngsters. One of these remembers with great clarity the day that the machine stuck and to the growing amazement of he and and his friends, produced no less than 19 bars of chocolate for one penny. All this proved too much for the lucky lads who were so captivated by the spectacle that they failed to detect the approach of an angry station master Parry. After a proper dressing down in his office, the boys' fathers were informed, and swift parental retribution ensured that soft chairs were in great demand for the next day or so!
P. W. Gray

The '54XX' class pannier tanks were a later development of the '2021s' with larger 5 ft 2 in diameter wheels, No. 2080, a Lydney loco, having been rewheeled in 1930 in a successful experiment prior to the first of the class being built the following year. However, the class did not make its appearance in the area until 1951 when it was used on both the Berkeley Road and Cinderford passenger services, and No. 5408 is shown here on a typical 1950s Forest of Dean branch auto-train.
Lens of Sutton

An unusual view of the station taken on 17th May 1948. The view is contemporary with that on page 348 and gives a good impression of the surrounding landscape. The rough ground in the right middle distance marks the site of the former Spero colliery, which had closed before the station was built, and the houses beyond this are the northern outskirts of Cinderford. Also visible are three sheds which are evidently recent additions to the goods yard. Unfortunately, once again nothing is known of their date of origin or use.   *L. E. Copeland*

An irregular manoeuvre about to take place, with '57XX' class pannier tank No. 8717 already partly inside the goods shed on an overcast day in 1962. In fact the goods shed headshunt had a noticeable gradient up to the buffer stops to enable loaded wagons and vans to roll back down to the goods shed by gravity alone, in order to avoid the need for motive power during unloading activities. From 1961, however, removal of the loco release crossover from the platform loop meant that an engine could only run round its train via the goods shed.

A. K. Pope

The station enjoys a welcome break from winter storms as it is bathed in strong sunlight on 5th March 1962. The number of delivery vehicles alongside the goods shed seems to indicate that the parcels service was still going strong at that date, although it had less than four years left to run. Also visible to the right of the access road is the petrol pump provided in March 1957 together with a 500 gallon tank which, since it does not appear in any contemporary photographs, was probably installed underground.   *A. K. Pope*

Cinderford goods shed was solidly constructed from Forest of Dean stone with a corrugated iron roof, and measured 60 ft x 33 ft 6 ins internally. The stonework of the eaves course was different to that of the office, the former appearing to be the same as the main structure, whilst the office eaves may be of Grinshill white sandstone like those of the station building. The main goods shed windows were of wrought iron whereas those in the office were wooden sash type, and all window cills were of blue brick. The end doors were originally of 2 inch deal planking and were approximately three quarters of the height of the opening with a spiked top rail to prevent illegal entry. By the late 1940s these had been replaced by the full height corrugated iron doors seen here and in the photograph opposite. Internally the goods shed possessed a centrally mounted 2 ton crane and a weighing machine. At the opposite end to the office was a timber lock-up with a book loft above which was reached by a portable ladder, and illumination was provided by large gas lamps. The office and goods shed were linked internally by a doorway, and a glazed hatchway next to this was presumably used to pass wagon labels and other paperwork.

                                                                                                                                        A. K. Pope

A final view of the station from the Valley Road overbridge as '57XX' class pannier tank No. 3675 shunts the yard on 29th October 1965, only two months before the end of steam haulage on the Forest of Dean branch. A wooden scotch block had been fitted across the platform line to stop accidental runaways of vehicles parked in the platform, and a notice warning of its presence appears in the foreground. The platform line no longer had a release crossover and had thus become a siding, but the expense of laying in a trap point was deemed unnecessary.

A. K. Pope

The area around the northern end of the station building was used from the early days as the site for a succession of small buildings and huts. Unfortunately, the history of these was not well recorded and the exact pattern of events is unclear. Of the three structures seen here, the coal store to the right of the group was the first to be built and was provided by 1902-3, lasting until closure. The building in the centre is the carpenters' shop seen in the view on page 329. By January 1944 it was disused and the Joint Committee agreed to adapt it for use as a garage for their motor lorry at an estimated cost of £30, and in August 1946 an expenditure of £10 was approved for doors and a lock for the 'garage'. The building on the left is the replacement of the linemen's hut seen on page 331, which was presumably removed after 1930 to make way for the brick-built structure seen in the lower view on page 347.   *A. K. Pope*

No. 8729 departs towards Cinderford Junction with a short freight on 4th June 1962.   *A. K. Pope*

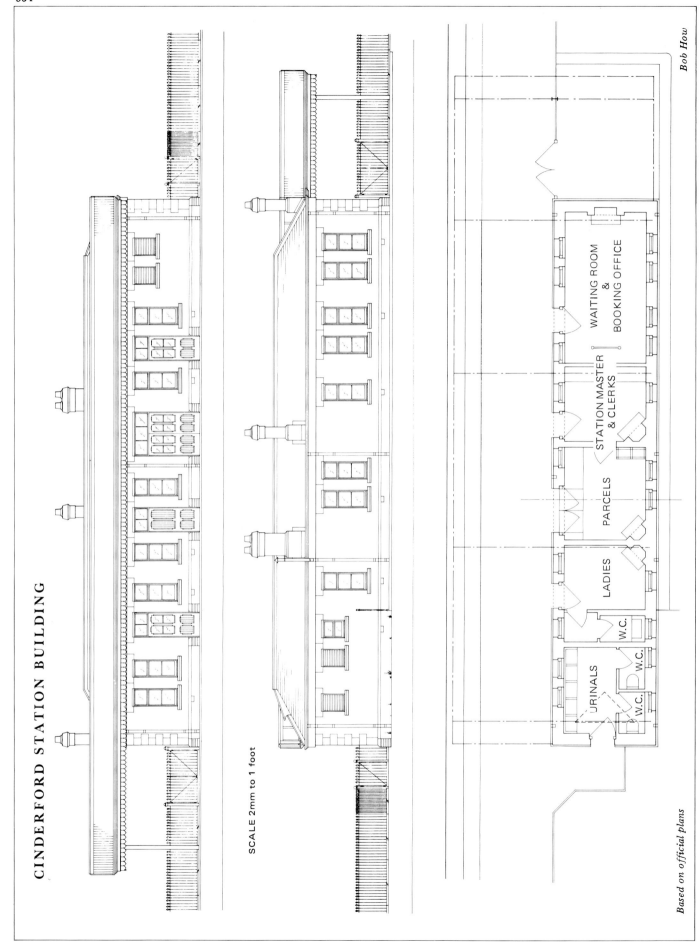

CINDERFORD STATION BUILDING

SCALE 2mm to 1 foot

WAITING ROOM & BOOKING OFFICE

STATION MASTER & CLERKS

PARCELS

LADIES

W.C.

URINALS

W.C.

W.C.

W.C.

Bob How

Based on official plans

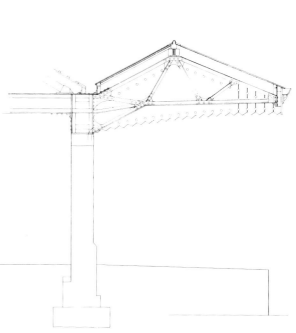

SCALE: 4mm to 1 foot

A. Attewell

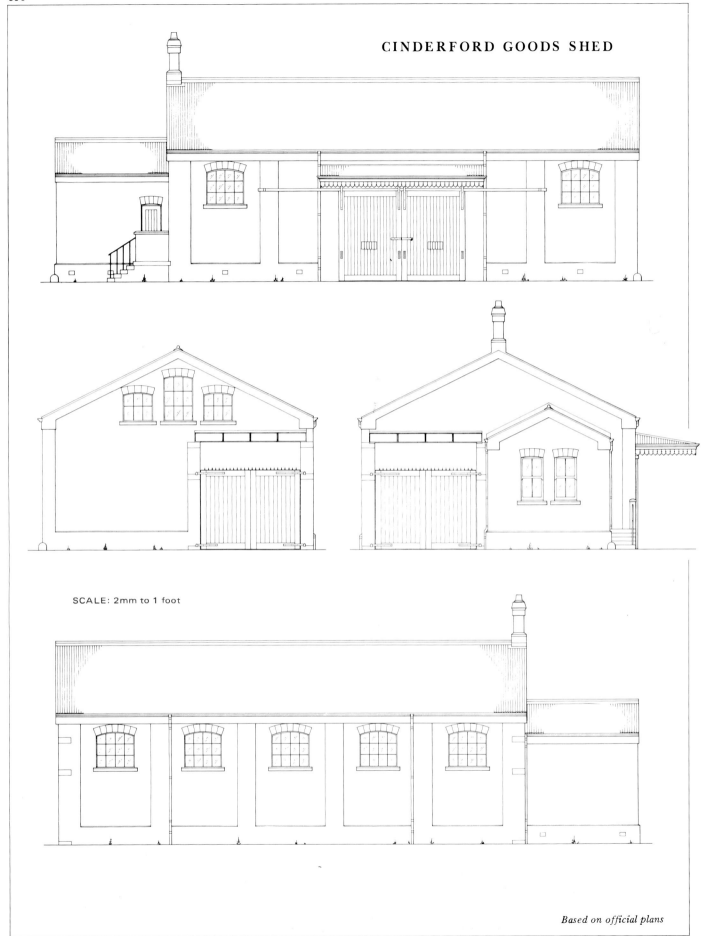

356

CINDERFORD GOODS SHED

SCALE: 2mm to 1 foot

Based on official plans

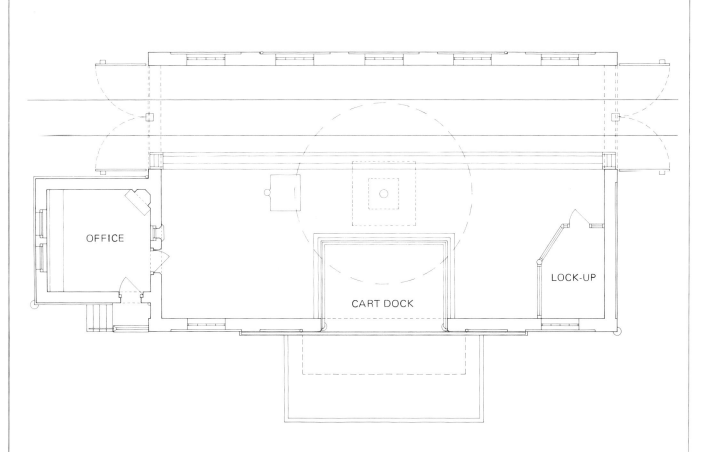

OFFICE

CART DOCK

LOCK-UP

SCALE: 2mm to 1 foot

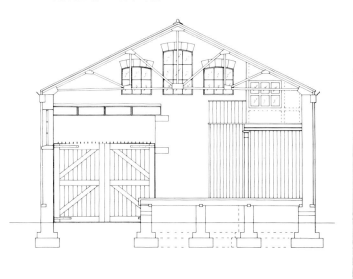

A. Attewell

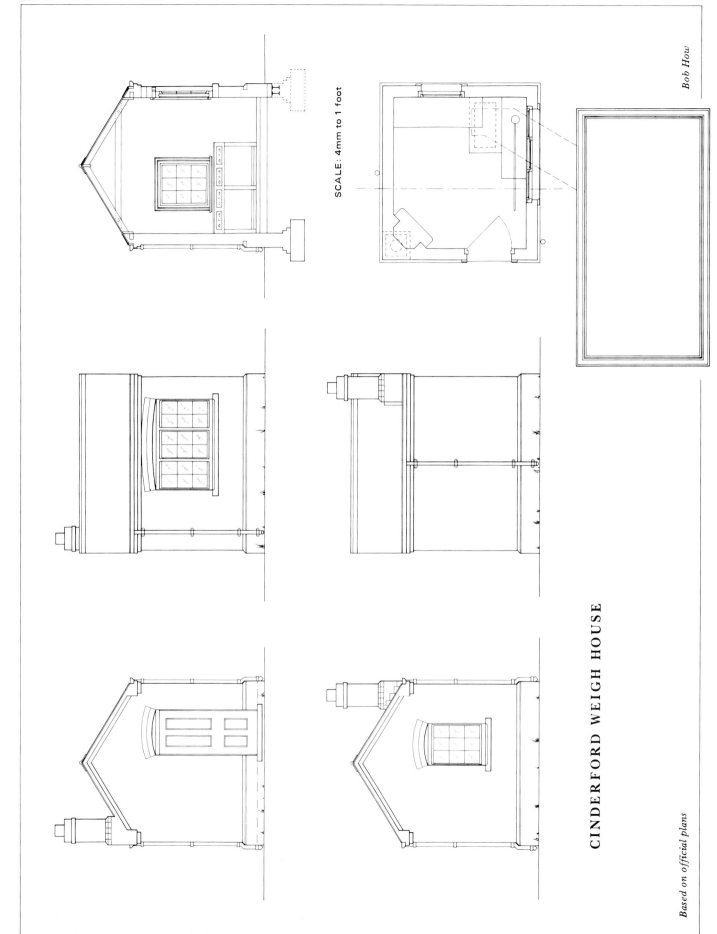

SCALE : 4mm to 1 foot

Bob How

CINDERFORD WEIGH HOUSE

Based on official plans

CINDERFORD BREWERY STORE

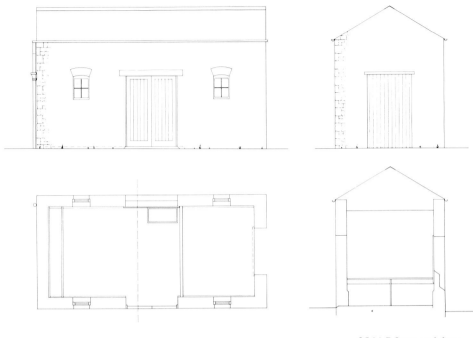

SCALE 2mm to 1 foot

Based on official sketch plan

Bob How

The building erected as a store for the Nailsworth Brewery Company was authorised in October 1900 and bore a strong 'family' resemblance to the adjacent goods shed, having a similar construction of stone with a corrugated iron roof. Ownership of the store is unclear as early records suggest that the plot of land was sold to the brewery company, but by 1913 a tenancy agreement is recorded. By 1930 the store had been converted to a stable and garage and had changed hands, Joint Committee minutes recording its purchase from the Cheltenham Original Brewery Company, and it is possible that Messrs. Smith, the cartage agents, had been using the building to house their horse dray for some time prior to this. Later still, the building was known to a former signal-man at Bilson Junction as the 'sugar shed', and it ultimately became known as the 'cement shed', although not used for this purpose during the final years. This view also shows clearly the windows in the northern end of the goods shed. *A. K. Pope*

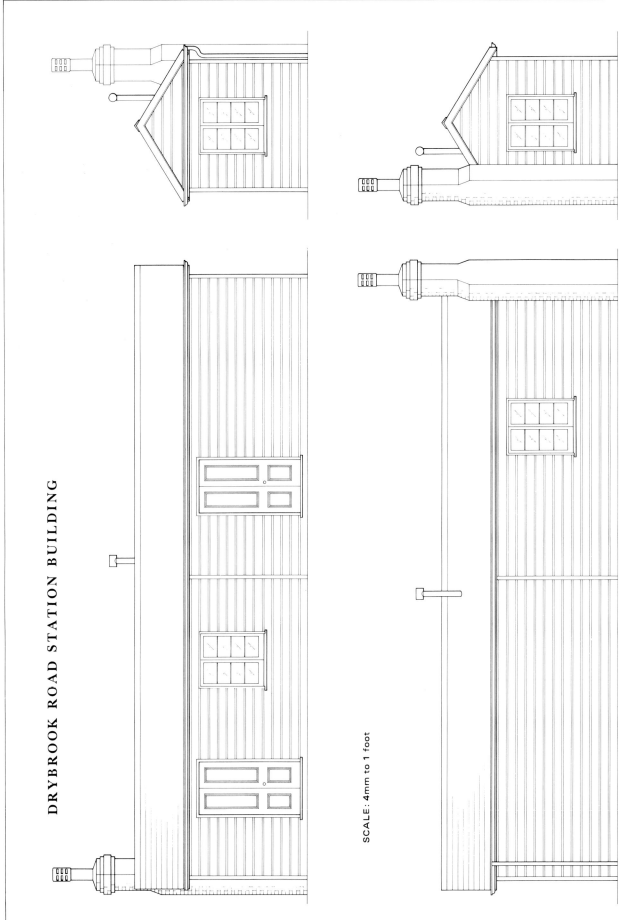

DRYBROOK ROAD STATION BUILDING

SCALE: 4mm to 1 foot

Bob How

Based on official leading dimensions and photographs

SPEECH HOUSE ROAD STATION BUILDING

SCALE — 4mm to 1 foot

Bob How

Based on official leading dimensions and photographs

SPEECH HOUSE ROAD GOODS SHED

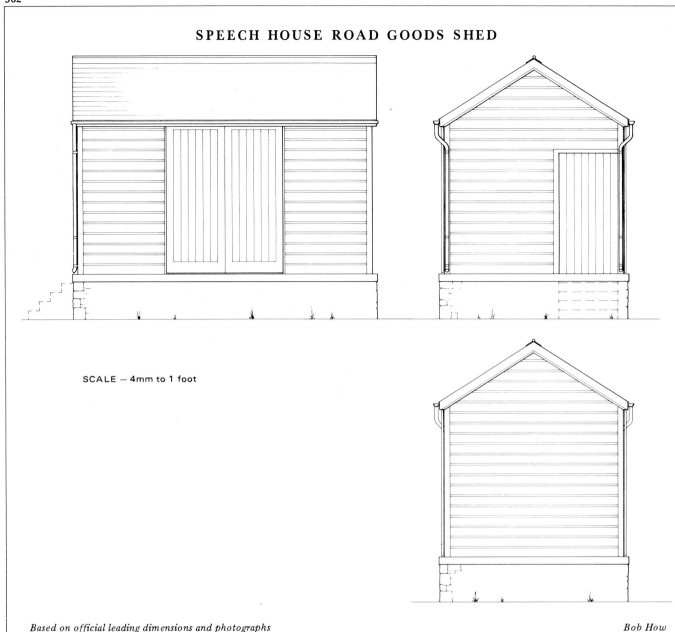

SCALE — 4mm to 1 foot

Based on official leading dimensions and photographs

Bob How

ACKNOWLEDGEMENTS

Very special thanks are due to Alec Pope to whom this volume is dedicated. Besides giving us complete freedom to raid his cupboards and pick his brains again, his trust, generosity and general easy-going and kindly nature have ensured an unfailing warm welcome in the Forest, always accompanied by a sincere smile. Many of the historic views of the area have come from his well-known family collection, supplemented by his own views of the railways in the Forest. We hope these pages bring back happy memories of Speech House Road and Serridge Junction where he spent many happy hours and took Ian for his first footplate ride.

As with Volume 1, we have again received great assistance from many people, some for the first time, but most for a second. Harry Paar, Peter Copeland and Rev. David Tipper have once again given us valuable assistance and advice, Peter's photographs again forming the backbone of this volume and providing many unique viewpoints. Keith Allford also kindly allowed us to raid his photographic collection which forms a superb record of the permanent way and signalling during the later years. On the industrial side Tony Sargeant and Ivor Brown have provided very useful information, especially on Cannop Colliery which they both knew well.

Particular thanks are also due to Roger Carpenter, Keith Waters and Tony Smith for many hours spent printing and copying photo-graphs and to Neil Parkhouse who once more allowed generous use of postcards from his extensive collection. Mike Christensen has kindly added his signalling expertise to our manuscript for a second time (at exceptionally short notice — again!) whilst Jim Imm, Cyril Trigg and Hedley Woodward have suffered more of our questions and continued to allow us an insight into their working days, which, besides the priviledge, has considerably enhanced the flavour of our text.

We should also like to thank Jack Aston, Gerry Beale, John Belcher, Maurice Billington, Jack Burrell, John Dagley-Morris, Roy Denison, S. Fletcher, Forest of Dean Newspapers Ltd., P. J. Garland, P. W. Gray, Eric Gwynne, J. James, Mrs. Knight, Lens of Sutton, John Mann, John Marshall, John Morris, Eric Parker, Mike Rees, John Rodway, Peter Skelton, Harry Townley, Frances Webb, Dr. D. V. Willetts and Norman Williams, David & Charles for permitting the use of L & GRP photographs, British Rail, the Public Record Office at Kew, the staff of Gloucester Public Library, the Dean Forest Mercury, Gloucester Railway Carriage & Wagon Co. Ltd. and finally, Clare, Chris and June again for typing, criticism and the usual moral support.